MW01491516

Jazz
June

ALSO BY CLIFFORD THOMPSON

Signifying Nothing: A Novel

Love for Sale and Other Essays

Twin of Blackness: A Memoir

What It Is: Race, Family, and One Thinking Black Man's Blues

Big Man and the Little Men: A Graphic Novel

SERIES EDITOR

Nicole Walker

SERIES ADVISORY BOARD

Steve Fellner
Kiese Laymon
Lia Purpura
Paisley Rekdal
Wendy S. Walters
Elissa Washuta

Jazz
June

A SELF-PORTRAIT IN ESSAYS

Clifford Thompson

The University of Georgia Press
ATHENS

Published by the University of Georgia Press
Athens, Georgia 30602
www.ugapress.org
© 2025 by Clifford Thompson
All rights reserved
Designed by Rebecca A. Norton
Set in 10.5 / 14 Minion Pro
Printed and bound by Sheridan Books, Inc.
The paper in this book meets the guidelines for
permanence and durability of the Committee on
Production Guidelines for Book Longevity of the
Council on Library Resources.

Most University of Georgia Press titles are
available from popular e-book vendors.

Printed in the United States of America
29 28 27 26 25 P 5 4 3 2 1

Library of Congress Control Number: 2025009792
ISBN: 9780820374642 (paperback: alk. paper)
ISBN: 9780820374659 (ebook)
ISBN: 9780820374666 (PDF)

For my mother and father

Contents

Acknowledgments

I am deeply grateful to Beth Snead and Sarah Shermyen of the University of Georgia Press and to my capable agent, Andrew Blauner.

Many thanks go to my old pal Charles Hawley for providing a valuable second pair of eyes on the manuscript. I am indebted as well to the editors of the following publications, where these essays first appeared: *Forum* magazine/The Honor Society of Phi Kappa Phi ("Tales from Washington," Winter 2021); the *Chicago Quarterly Review* ("Ming Yang Fu," vol. 33, 2021); *Speak* ("Equinox," June 2018); *AGNI* ("Summer of '83," Fall 2019, and "Seventeen Notes on Singing," November 25, 2019); *Mr. Beller's Neighborhood* and *The Coal Hill Review* (the two halves of "New York in Two Reels," February 2019 and November 2019); the *American Book Review* ("Blues for Mister Stanley," Winter 2021); the *Los Angeles Review of Books* ("Eric Garner and Me," March 13, 2015); and *Writing the Virus*, published by StatORec and edited by Andrea Scrima and David Dario Winner ("Rooms and Clarinets"). "Interlude: On Film and Romance" originally appeared as "Interlude" in my memoir *Twin of Blackness*, published by Autumn House Press in 2015; it has been revised and is reprinted with the permission of The Permissions Company, LLC on behalf of Autumn House, autumnhouse.org. I want to say a special thanks to Gerald Early, the founding editor of *The Common Reader*, Washington University in Saint Louis's Journal of the Essay ("Life with Rodents," January 4, 2018, and "Long Red Monte Carlo," March 25, 2020), who has a peculiar knack for getting me to write pieces I wouldn't necessarily think of on my own. And I want to say an extra-special thanks to Wendy Lesser, the founding editor of *The Threepenny Review*, who has given my work a home for a quarter-century now ("The Moon, the World, the Dream," Spring 2017; "Jazz June," Spring 2016; "On the Bus," Spring 2015; "Cities, Bulls, and the Boy at Seventeen," Fall 2014; "On Rivers," Spring 2014; "The Home of Two Cliffs," Spring 2021; "La Bohème," Spring 2022; "Out of the Past," Spring 2018; "Summer of '07," Fall 2015; "The Quiet Dark," Spring 2023).

Many years ago, someone asked me how it was possible to be a writer while raising a family. I don't remember my answer, but at this point I wonder what, without a family, I would have to write *about*; that is how much marriage and fatherhood have informed the way I look at life. And so I want, finally, to thank the members of my family—both the one I helped to raise and the one that raised me.

Preface

In choosing the subtitle for *Jazz June*, I considered but rejected the word "memoir," which suggests to me an overarching narrative, a single story. While this is undeniably a book about my life, my life is not a single story, because no one's is. To be sure, one can tease from one's life a central tale with an underlying theme, and many have done just that, very successfully, but I have tried to do something else here. It seems to me that a person's life comprises many, many moments that, individually and collectively, reveal that individual and their views and way of being in the world. These are often not the so-called watershed moments but the in-between times, not defining but emblematic. They are the unrequited crushes, middle-of-the-night reflections, quiet epiphanies, and other small occasions that make up a life and that, examined together, amount to a portrait. That examination is what I have tried to do with *Jazz June*.

This is not to say that no common themes emerge from the twenty-two pieces collected here. *Jazz June* is about childhood and youth; family; fatherhood; friendship; romantic relationships, real or hoped for; literary ambition; the arts (specifically literature and comics, film and TV, jazz and soul); aging; and, inevitably, because I am a Black American, what we like to call race.

For the most part, the essays here are arranged chronologically according to their starting points. In the first, I recall an event that occurred when I was five years old; the second finds me at age eight; and so on, into late middle age. Frequently, however, an essay that begins at an early point in my life will jump forward in time. In this way, I think I have created a work that operates as a kind of photographic negative of real life. Whereas, in life, we occupy a continual present while our minds frequently return to the past, this book reaches into the past while making return trips to the present, or near-present. The book is divided into two sections, "Washington" and "New York," because if my life were boiled down to its essence, that would be the story: I started in one place, and made my way to the other.

One final note. I refer often in *Jazz June* to my two daughters, one of whom now identifies as nonbinary. Most of the essays were written when I still thought of my child as a daughter, and for that reason, I decided to keep the "daughter" references. Still, I wanted to check with my child to see if that was okay. They very graciously supported that choice. When I wrote in an email that I could mention the issue in my preface, they wrote back, "It's your work, Pa. Do whatever makes sense." That is what I've tried to do, when it comes to this issue and the arrangement of the book as a whole. I hope that you enjoy *Jazz June* and that it brings an occasional smile to your face.

Clifford Thompson

BROOKLYN, NEW YORK
MARCH 2024

Washington

The Moon, the World, the Dream

ON FAMILY AND

HIDDEN WORLDS

I grew up in a Washington, D.C., neighborhood called Deanwood, where daily life did not involve a sense of living in the most important city on Earth. Everyone in Deanwood was Black, working class to working poor, some living in housing projects, others— including my family—in private semidetached brick homes. We went to school or work in the mornings, came home in the evenings; no one traveled far, for their jobs or anything else, the exceptions mostly being trips "down the country" to families' even more insular places of origin in Virginia, say, or North Carolina. In December, in school, we put on Christmas programs because it was assumed, rightly, that everyone was a Christian in our world—for us, the only world there was.

In my memory this sleepiness was at its sweetest in the spring and summer, when the front doors of houses up and down my street were routinely left open to let the breeze in, when, as darkness came, people rocked on metal gliders on their small porches, when sounds were mostly of cicadas whirring and crickets chirping and the occasional car passing with a lazy roar up the street, when the only other movement was of moths floating near the yellow glow of the streetlamps.

On the one such night that I'm recalling, in the warm months of 1968, when I was five, the insularity of my world suffered a brief, bizarre jolt. My brother, then nineteen, was beside me on the porch and remembers what I remember, which for nearly half a century was all that kept me from thinking of it as a dream.

We were gazing at the full moon. Then, beside it, part of the sky began to change color, as if an invisible dial was spinning and painting as it went around, until at the end of a second there was a perfect white sphere. Where a moment before there had been one moon, we now saw two.

Small children are, for the most part, rational beings, operating in the world based on their feelings but also on what they've learned. When children see things they want, they simply grab them until they are told, and remember, not to. When pleased that things they've said have made others laugh, they'll say them again, soon filing away the lesson that funny lines almost never work a second time. And when confronted with things that go radically against their learned notions of how the world ought to work, children, like adults, become upset, even frightened.

Seeing what seemed to me the formation of a second moon, I ran screaming into our little house—trying, no doubt incoherently, to talk about what I'd witnessed. I don't recall that I was upset for very long. If, just beyond the screen door, the world was turning upside down, here in the house everything was as it ought to have been. There was my teenaged older sister, sitting calmly in a chair beside the dining room table; there, behind her, was my mother, applying a black, smoking-hot iron comb to my sister's head; here was the familiar crackling sound and the old smell of singed hair. Probably the TV was on. I felt safe again, back in the world I knew, the one where I was the lone small child in a household of two parents, a grandmother, and grown or near-grown siblings who would let no harm come to me.

Clearly, though, I've never forgotten that other feeling.

If fear—and the accompanying fight-or-flight—is our first natural response to the unfamiliar, our second has to involve jokes. The most common response when I shared the second-moon story with friends recently was that I'd had too much of my beloved bourbon (never mind that I was five years old at the time I'm recalling). In case you're having doubts of your own, please know that I have never taken a mind-expanding drug or been diagnosed with a mental illness, and unless you count setting out to become a writer, I've never been known for giving way to delusions. (And even with regard to that, a good friend told me once long ago that the problem with my becoming a writer was that I'm "not crazy enough.")

Plus, my story is corroborated by probably the most sober person I know: my big brother. "I was almost twenty, and it unsettled me," he said recently, "so I can believe you were scared." His explanation for what we saw? When I mention it, every few years or so, his response has been reassuringly consistent, if a little light on detail: "They"—whoever "they" are—"were testing chemicals in the sky." That was all I had to go on until recently, when I finally decided to dig a little deeper on my own.

I am hardly a conspiracy theorist, but I've long been intrigued by things that shake up my view of the world around me—specifically, things that awaken my sense that what most of us see makes up very little of what there is, that there's much more going on around us than we know. Some of the movies I've found memorable—Sidney Lumet's *Q&A*, Martin Scorsese's *The Departed*, and, for its Nazi submarine sequence, Woody Allen's *Radio Days*—appeal to my sense of a scarcely believable reality beneath the usual veneer, especially when it comes to human activity.

What I witnessed from my porch as a five-year-old, while not related to human interaction, definitely shook my settled view of things, an understanding based in part on the utter predictability of the night sky. The irony is that the world I lived in, the ground I walked on, the moon I saw at night were all formed by events so fantastic, and taking place on so indescribably large a scale, that the average adult mind—let alone the mind of a five-year-old—could not wrap itself around them.

The leading theory of the moon's formation is that, longer ago than most of us can comprehend, another young planet collided with our own, its core merged with our planet's, parts of its crust were knocked loose along with parts of Earth's, and the loose sections fused into one with the heat of the impact as they spun away from the two now-joined planets to become our moon. In the summer of 1969, roughly a year after the fantastic thing I saw in the sky, humans went for the first time to this moon. I have very dim memories of watching the coverage on TV, and I still have a drawing of the astronauts I did in whatever summer school I was attending then. What now strikes me as significant about the moon landing—beyond the obvious—is that, in light of the theory of the moon's formation, you could say the astronauts were not only going to a new world: in the most concrete sense, they were returning home.

The moon, of course, continues to orbit Earth, rotating, as it does so, in such a way that we always see more or less the same side of it; it has been estimated that only 59 percent of the moon is visible, and not all of that is visible at once. One great thing about writing nonfiction is that you are free to *explain* your metaphors, and these facts about the moon seem to me applicable to all kinds of things. Recently, my younger daughter—the result, you might say, of the collision/merger of her mother and me—spun so far away from us as to enroll at a small midwestern college. Since she left, she has taken to emailing us videos of herself talking. In one of them, with her black-framed glasses, head wrap, and light brown skin, she looked strikingly like Zadie Smith. But even more striking, for me, was that I was suddenly looking at a woman. This was not the little person holding my hand and toddling beside me en route to Park Slope's Third Street Playground, the person about whom I knew, or thought I knew, everything; here was a young adult with as great a store of private knowledge as I have, one who shows me certain sides of herself but not others, and if I knew 59 percent of what was going on with her, I would know far too much. ("Don't you ever ask them why / If they told you, you would cry . . .")

Fifty-nine percent, of course, is more than I'll ever know about what's going on with the rest of the world, which brings me back to hidden human activity and forward to something I witnessed, not as a five-year-old, but as a young single man living in Harlem. One weekday afternoon in the late 1980s, I was in Midtown Manhattan, on the first floor of the Citicorp building, with its shops and scores of people walking this way and that. I was relaxing with a cup of coffee, thinking and staring at nothing, when two men entered my line of vision from opposite directions, one of them carrying a shopping bag; the men passed each other with no acknowledgment, without breaking stride or turning their heads even slightly—but one of them dropped an object I couldn't see into the shopping bag of the other man.

To one extent or another, we create for ourselves the lives we envision, which means that each of us lives in a world of his or her imagination. The intrusion of another world into our own—analogous to the process that likely formed the moon—can be unsettling, for good or ill, on a small or large scale: seeing something strange in the sky, witnessing a mysterious handoff, falling in love.

For glimpses into other worlds, we need not turn to the heavens, or even to other people. There is the land of sleep. Except for my brother's presence on the porch that night in 1968, as I have said, I would have thought I dreamed what I saw; a second moon would not have been out of place in dreams, where one's own mind becomes a stranger, speaking of incomprehensible things in a language we cannot translate back in the waking world.

Here is Marcel Proust, in *In Search of Lost Time*, on the subject of dreams:

> Our perceptions are so overloaded, each of them blanketed by a
> superimposed counterpart which doubles its bulk and blinds it to
> no purpose, that we are unable even to distinguish what is happen-
> ing in the bewilderment of awakening . . . that murky obscurity in
> which reality is no more translucent than in the body of a porcu-
> pine, and our all but non-existent perception may perhaps give us
> an idea of the perception of certain animals.

And:

In the chariot of sleep, we descend into depths in which memory can no longer keep up with it, and on the brink of which the mind has been obliged to retrace its steps.

And:

Sleep bore him so far away from the world inhabited by memory and thought, through an ether in which he was alone, more than alone, without even the companionship of self-perception, he was outside the range of time and its measurements.

Proust was a man who bent language to his will, whom words served as they served no one else—and even he doesn't quite nail it. Where Proust falls short, I would be wise not to try, except to say that if describing what happens in certain areas of sleep is beyond the power of the planet's preeminent master of language, then it is because there simply is no human language adequate to the task. Sleep thought is based on the logic of the alien within ourselves.

All we can do, then, is try to figure out some of what's going on in the world of waking life.

Several months ago I talked with my brother about that night in 1968. He said something I didn't recall his having said before: that prior to our second-moon sighting, there was a mention in the newspaper or on TV or radio about atmospheric tests. Armed with that knowledge, I spent a recent summer afternoon at the main branch of the New York Public Library, searching through the *Washington Post* database to see where the terms "atmospheric," "testing," "chemicals," and "NASA" appeared in articles published in the spring and summer of 1968, hoping to find a connection to what I witnessed. I came up empty. Disappointed, I went home and, in a spirit of what-have-I-got-to-lose, posted on Facebook a description of my childhood experience and a call for advice on how to solve this mystery. Amid the jokey responses was a suggestion that I contact a man named Derrick Pitts at a science museum called the Franklin Institute in Philadelphia. That turned out to be a very good idea.

I learned from Derrick Pitts, an African American and the

Franklin Institute's chief astronomer, that during the period of my second-moon sighting, NASA routinely conducted atmospheric tests involving what are called sounding rockets—which carry scientific instruments into space—launched from the Wallops Flight Facility, not far from Washington. Next, I sent an email to Wallops, whose news chief, Keith Koehler, informed me that what I saw sounded like a "vapor tracer experiment using a sounding rocket." According to information on the NASA page to which he sent me a link, vapor tracers are injections into the atmosphere of materials that either luminesce or scatter sunlight in order to reveal . . . I'm still working on understanding what.

One vapor, lithium, turns bright red when used at night; another, barium, is used only near sunset or sunrise and shows up as purplish-red. But then there is trimethylaluminum (TMA), which turns white—and which sounds like it might have produced what my brother and I saw. According to the NASA web page, "TMA releases are most often used to study the neutral winds in the lower ionosphere at night at altitudes of 100 miles (160 kilometers) or less." Searching online for a definition of "neutral winds," I found a paragraph of impenetrable science-speak; after emailing two people in the field, I got back responses that seemed to me like descriptions of two different phenomena. I thought of how my late mother used to respond to unhelpful explanations: *Don't know no more'n I did before.*

So I'm left with three problems. The first—that I don't have a grasp of what neutral winds are—is perhaps not a real problem, since I don't know that even a definitive, plain-English explanation would benefit me much in the end. The second is that what I read about white TMA vapors, which is probably as good an explanation as I will ever have of what I saw, doesn't sound exactly like what I saw—the amorphous vapor cloud lacking the crispness of that quickly formed sphere I recall so clearly. So did I witness something else? Or could it be that forty-eight years have distorted my childhood memory just a little? Do I think that the TMA vapor experiment accounts for what I witnessed? Let's say I'm 59 percent sure. More, even.

The third problem is that having (maybe, probably, I think) at last solved this mystery, I am presented with the one behind it. Why did I want so much to know the answer? Why have I talked about the subject so much to my wife and daughters that now, when I mention it, they smile, pat my shoulder, and head off to see if that pot of water is boiling yet? Maybe it's that having crossed the line of fifty—having nearly reached an age my father never saw—has given me the feeling that some mysteries of my life have to be solved soon, if at all; and maybe the question of what I saw when I was five, not critically important on its face, is a stand-in for something else I don't know about myself—a pretty benign substitute, as these things go. No doubt, having trophy wives, fancy cars, and other cliché trappings of midlife crises are not what aging sufferers seek so much as seeing themselves *with* the wives and the cars; discovering what they themselves are like under these new and different circumstances; finding out at last, in this big, endlessly mystifying world, who they are. By shaking things up and seeing what remains in place, we hope to discover what in us is permanent, or what we've merely never bothered to toss away. If that is the real question, maybe I found part of the answer as a small boy. In a moment when the world around me suddenly seemed as scary, crazy, and unpredictable as any movie, as ill-intentioned as any conspiracy, as unfathomable as any dream, I went running toward my family, and I wanted to describe what I'd seen. At the moment when a long-standing mystery was introduced, a small area of darkness turned to light.

Tales from Washington

ON FAMILY,

FIGHTS, HOME,

AND THE BOYS OF YOUTH

When I think of my friend Simon, who is both an engineer and a captain in the New York Fire Department, the word "capable" comes to mind. Simon is a man who knows how to do things, how things work, how to get from here to there. Among other things, he seems to have a complete map in his head of the city where he was born and raised. Simon also has a good sense of humor and a wealth of stories, some funny, some sad, from his work with the fire department. I jokingly call him "New York's only firefighter," because it seems to me that where there's smoke, there's Simon. 9/11? He was there. When a famous writer who was an acquaintance of mine had a fire in his Manhattan apartment, guess who showed up to pull him out.

Simon is, to put this another way, several things that I am not. My life has been fascinating (though mainly to me) because of an inner journey, a story over which magazine reporters would not fight, over which Comedy Central audience members would not gasp for air. I am capable—capable of spotting a dangling modifier or explaining why you shouldn't describe something as "highly unique"—but if you need a lift to the airport, call Lyft, not me: I have what I am convinced will be diagnosed in the future as a disability but for now just gets me laughed at, which is not a bad sense of direction but a sense of misdirection. I'm the kind of person who can get lost in a restaurant on the way back from the men's room. My cousin, a close friend, once compared me to "a homing pigeon on LSD." As for knowing how things work ... whenever our super comes up to fix the toilet or kitchen sink, my wife shows him what's wrong while I stand in the living room gazing at our bookshelves.

All of this may shed some light on why I went into a mild panic at something Simon told me several years ago. Returning from a trip to Washington, D.C., my hometown, Simon said, "I want to go there with *you* sometime. I want to see *your* Washington." How, touched though I was, could I explain that on such a trip he would see Washington through tears of boredom, that I would die of embarrassment as I got us lost en route to places where nothing happened? How, instead, could I share "my" Washington, the one where nobody can go anymore, the one whose map I carry around in my head?

Having now spent over half my life in New York, where every place, every place, has a name, I find it strange today that the Washington neighborhood where I grew up was never called anything, at least not that I was aware of back then. (I learned only as an adult that I spent my childhood in Deanwood.) I used to hear my mother tell people that we lived in "Far Northeast," but that designation covered a handful of neighborhoods. One thing those neighborhoods had in common: it was nothing to go days without seeing a white person, except on TV, and even TV showed only certain kinds. Once, when I was six or seven, which made it 1969 or 1970, I tagged along with one of my (much) older sisters on a shopping trip way across the city to Georgetown. On the way back, at the bus stop on the sun-dappled street where we waited, another person waited, too, reading a newspaper while I stared at ... him? The beard and mustache suggested a man, but the long blond hair he wore in a ponytail like the girls on that new show *The Brady Bunch* threw the whole thing into confusion. Who, what, was this person? Where did he come from, and where was he going?

A bus ride, then another bus ride, and home . . . Across the street from us, a little to the left, a set of cracked concrete steps ran up the front of a grassy mound, on top of which was a falling-down wooden shotgun house. It was there, in late 1971 or early '72, when I was eight, that Kevin Stewart moved in with his family. Kevin was a short boy with kinky, close-cropped brown hair, reddish-tan skin, and a wide nose with oddly thin, delicate, sculpted-looking nostrils. When he turned up in Mrs. Thompson's (no relation to me) third-grade class, I showed him around, telling him who was who, and we became friends. Kevin was quiet—at first. That changed when he fell in with a set of boys rougher than me (those were not hard to find), becoming something like their prince.

"And how did he treat you after that?" This question came about a dozen years later from the girlfriend to whom I told a version of this story. Moving around a lot as a child, she explained, had taught her that the kids who were nice in the beginning usually turned out to be the friendless outcasts of the class.

She had nailed me . . . sort of. It was true that I didn't have many friends in school, but I couldn't be called an outcast; my reputation for smarts brought me too much respect for that. Whether or not because I was smart, Kevin kept a spot in his heart for me, still coming over to my house sometimes. My relationship to Kevin became like that of a wife to a loving but philandering husband. The analogy is more apt than it may sound, because there was an element in all this that, it seems to me now, was not far removed from sex. Kevin would form friendships with one boy at a time, each so intense that it inevitably led to an equally passionate fistfight—as if this was Kevin's way of getting to know his friends more intimately, of making love to them. A fight between him and Julius Chappelle broke out near me in Miss Taylor's fourth-grade class, the two of them on the floor with their arms hooked around each other's necks, chairs falling over, both boys' eyes shut tight with fury, blood darkening a small patch of Julius's hair. A short time later I saw them laughing together. (Things never reached that stage between Kevin and me. Like other boys, he seemed afraid to even consider fighting me, not because I would have beaten him but because it would have been easy to beat me—easy like all tickets to hell.) I wonder now if Kevin's tendencies really did represent the earliest stages of his sexual energy, and I imagine him fifteen years after I knew him, acting out the same pattern with women (or men? or both?): an intense courtship, then sex, and then on to somebody else. As I have observed over the years, people tend to become early on what they will more or less remain.

I saw Kevin take part in one fight that, by contrast, underscored the nature of the others. At one point, across the street and up the block from our house, there was a construction site where another house was being built. The site, with its great mounds of hard dirt, was a fun place to play. I was there one warm day with some boys from school when Kevin showed up. I never got many details, but it came out that he and a second boy had a beef with two other guys, and the construction site was where they had decided to settle matters. Another boy, let's call him Freddie, came along shortly after Kevin, and the two began to box. Gone from Kevin's movements was the passionate anger, that flip side of love, with which he battled his friends; these were pure tactics. About halfway through the fight, to my surprise, Freddie leaned forward and put his hands on his knees, resting, and Kevin—I'll never forget this—did the same; rather than plowing forward, taking advantage of his enemy's exhaustion, and finishing him off, this fifth-grade boy waited like a professional boxer monitored by an unseen referee, at one moment looking toward Freddie with a total absence of anger, gauging his readiness patiently, almost with sympathy. When Freddie stood erect again and put up his guard, Kevin raised his own wide fists, soon finding the opening he'd waited for and ending the fight with one flawless punch. I heard Kevin say to someone as he walked away, "I did my part," and I saw Freddie with his head tilted back, a large, thick, bottom-weighted dollop of blood falling from his nose and a curiously vacant expression on his face, as if he were thinking of something else entirely.

When the house was finally built on the construction site, the Glover family moved in. The son of the family was a stocky boy of about my age who was introduced to me, or introduced himself, as Warner. The kids I grew up with, though, didn't know what to do with "Warner," and so in the neighborhood his name, for all practical purposes, became "Warren." Hearing *everybody* call him that, and hearing the poor guy answer to it, overrode my knowledge of his actual name—to the point where, phoning his house once for some reason, I asked the woman who answered if Warren was home. I got no reply, no "Hold on, please," no "Can I tell him who's calling?" There was only silence, which, after the next sound I heard, I interpreted as disgust. Mrs. Glover must have held the phone—with its idiot caller—away from her, because her voice, while clear, sounded far off as she shouted, *"War-NER!"* I wanted more than anything in that moment to get Warner's mother back on the phone, to explain that I really *had* known her son's true name, that *I* wasn't like the other knuckleheads in this neighborhood. When I recall this now, I think several things. First, why did I care so much what this woman, whom I had never met, thought of me? And yet—see my theory re: Kevin Stewart—have I really changed? What is behind the act of writing an essay for publication if not a desire for strangers' admiration? Finally, that little episode was an early lesson, though I didn't think of it this way at the time, in the importance of keeping sight of what I know and believe; because it sometimes happens, in matters great and small, that a lot of people have it all wrong.

My sister Phyllis—whom I had accompanied to Georgetown the day I saw the bearded person with the ponytail—was the director of a summer day camp held in the basement of nearby St. Luke's Catholic Church. That was how I happened to attend the camp, where I spent five happy summers beginning when I was seven. The basement had a vast expanse of alternating red and white floor tiles (no doubt it wouldn't seem so vast now), with tables in the back for reading, writing, and arts and crafts and a stage in front, where our talent show took place at the end of each summer. Every Wednesday we went by bus on field trips, often to the Smithsonian; Phyllis and I still talk about the lunches we packed for those trips—invariably sandwiches of Underwood deviled ham on Wonder Bread, a steady diet of which would be the end of me today.

The pastor of St. Luke's was Father Miller, a middle-aged white man with a big round head and pale blond hair. One day Father Miller learned that someone had started a fire in the basement bathroom. Standing in the middle of the floor, he gave a talk to the lot of us, kids and counselors alike. I don't remember his words so much as his angry red and white face, but I can still hear the last thing he said: "If I find out who did it, I'll rip his ear off!" I know now, of course, and I suppose I knew then, that no one was going to lose a body part (though if the culprit had been revealed before Father Miller at that moment, who knows). But merely hearing this priest say those words shocked me. He stood, after all, for Christianity, which to me meant turning the other cheek, forgiving those who have wronged us seventy-times-seven times, loving others no matter what they did. Here was my first illustration of a truth that can be applied to everything from office life to the judicial system to the fall of communism: that no matter how good or well-intended a system or philosophy may be, it is the creation of—and, worse, in the hands of—human beings, which means that it will never work perfectly, that sometimes it will not work at all. For better or worse, for better *and* worse, people are not ideals but human beings.

In later years, summer would consist of perspiring in my shirt collar on the way to and from the office, managing maybe one trip to the beach, blinking twice, and realizing with a sigh that next week is September. In the St. Luke's days, when time was suspended, summer meant kickball games in the empty church parking lot, chatter and laughter amid Elmer's-glue-and-Popsicle-stick projects, knobby-kneed kids on stage singing pop hits whose recorded versions whispered from the record players behind them—all that, and the nameless yearning from being around all those girls at a time when I knew nothing about sex and not much more about love.

But there were many other moments, not of yearning but of contentment. In a certain room at the back of the house, a window gave a view of the Lincoln Heights housing projects but also, mostly, of trees, with their endless sunlit leaves in the summertime. At night in my small bedroom, in the front of the house, I would hear the occasional sound of a car passing leisurely up the street, a slow whoosh that greeted, somehow encompassed, us all—my parents and siblings and me, my grandmother, Kevin Stewart's family and Warner Glover's—the sound leaving me relaxed as it receded into the night and I closed my eyes . . .

It was easy to feel, in those moments of contentment, that life would remain as it was: that my brother and sisters would stay under my parents' roof, that my parents themselves would both remain alive and in that house, going to work and reading the paper and drinking instant coffee, that I would be in the capable hands of my whole family until . . . well, until a time I couldn't imagine. Soon I would not have to imagine it. But I like to remember that contented boy in his bedroom. Just for a moment, why don't we leave him there.

Ming Yang Fu, or Seeking Words at Age Thirteen

ON THE BOYS OF YOUTH,

FIGHTS, FAMILY, HOME,

COMICS, WRITING, RACE,

AND ROMANTIC YEARNING

1. BIRTHDAY

"I'm thirteen years old," I said aloud to myself, rising up on my elbows on my little bed, in my tiny room with its pale yellow walls. Near the head of the bed, the window framed the view more familiar to me than the outside of my own house: the red A-frame across the street, sitting atop a grassy mound on the corner. (Next to it was the falling-down house where Kevin Stewart lived.) Years earlier, when my brother—fourteen years older than I am—told me that Jesus was coming back one day, I had pictured Him walking quietly around that corner, alone and unceremoniously, with his long brown hair and beard, in his robe and sandals, arms raised in greeting. I wondered what he would say.

My mother sorted mail on the night shift at the post office. She walked in the front door downstairs at about the time I woke up and announced to myself that I was thirteen. Her mother, white-haired and all but deaf, turning eighty-two in exactly a week, had been up for hours, making herself butter-soaked toast in an aluminum pie plate in the broiler and loading great heaps of sugar into her coffee.

I went downstairs. The three of us sat around our dining room table. My grandmother, in a blue sleeveless housedress and one of the two or three cardigan sweaters she wore year-round, drank the last of the coffee she had perked, not hearing how loudly she slurped. My mother drank instant coffee. I ate cereal. My mother and I talked, intermittently, desultorily. Am I a bad writer if I admit that I have no idea what we talked about? The only one of those morning exchanges I remember is from the previous fall, when I had explained to Ma, tears forming in my eyes, why I had a lump on my head. She listened with calm and detachment to this story, which ended with me unconscious. Ma was fifty-one years old, and her husband was dead; she was responsible for her aged mother and had been for decades, would be for the rest of my grandmother's life and all but the last few of her own; and she pulled the night shift at the post office. As the general of our household, in the long slog of a battle that was her life, she seemed to view the problems of an enlisted man like me from a great height. That's not to say they weren't important to her. In the days after hearing my story, she gathered contact information for teachers at my old elementary school who would vouch for me if there should ever be a question of who was at fault, me or the boy I had gotten tangled up with. There was no question at all about that, and it was hardly the issue; but Ma was doing what she knew how to do. And at the breakfast table she gave me this, saying, despite all the evidence, "You're a pretty tough guy."

That, as I say, was the previous fall. The morning of my birthday—which I see from the internet was a Wednesday—I'm sure I got cards and presents from my mother and grandmother, because I did every year. I am also sure that when I left the table and got ready to go to school, my stomach was in a clench, because that's how it felt every morning.

I walked up our block of red brick semidetached houses. I crossed at the corner. At the opposite corner was Anthony Wilson's house. I went up the front steps.

Anthony was light-skinned, with brown kinky hair. Though Anthony and I were never exactly friends, his path and mine intertwined at various points in our lives. Years earlier, beginning as seven-year-olds, we had attended the same summer day camp, the one where my sister was the head counselor; Anthony would tell jokes that made the rest of us cry with laughter, jokes so funny to us because they made absolutely no sense, as if—and this may have been the case—Anthony didn't know what a joke *was*, but simply imitated the form, like a person who doesn't know French speaking random syllables with a Parisian accent. A joke might go like this. Q: What did the bird bring back to the nest? A (spoken by Anthony with a broad smile and mischief in the knit of his eyebrows): Ketchup, and mustard, and . . . By the following summer Anthony had gained an understanding of jokes but had lost something too. We begged him to tell some of his jokes, whereupon he looked confused for a moment and then told one we all knew from TV. (Q: What's the best way to catch a squirrel? A: Climb a tree and act like a nut.)

My picking Anthony up on the way to school in the mornings had to have been our families' idea, a way for us to form a needed bond in that first year of junior high. Like Anthony's old jokes, this morning routine was all form and no content. We had little to say to each other, even when we were talking. Today I cannot recall a single thing we said as we walked; I could make up a representative conversation, but that's exactly what I would be doing. I do, though, remember one morning, because it so perfectly captured our relationship. I went to his door; he came out. For some reason, neither of us said "Hey" or "Morning" or whatever we usually said. Without a word, we went down to the sidewalk. And thus began our game: how far could we go without saying anything? All the way to school? And, in fact, we made it. At the front door of Kelly Miller Junior High School, Anthony headed off toward his homeroom, I toward mine. In that year's most eloquent communication between us, we had not exchanged a word.

2. SUMMER

My friend Trevor Sampson lived down the street. Trevor, who was my age, skinny like me, had come with his family from South America several years earlier; I didn't know enough, or it didn't occur to me, to ask which country they had come from, and to this day I don't know. Like me, Trevor had two older sisters and an older brother, but unlike my siblings, they were teenagers and still lived at home. I never heard the Sampson family speak a language other than English, which they spoke with an accent. Trevor himself had a few speech patterns that as far as I could tell were all his own. He would start many sentences, for example, with *soon*: "Soon Cliff, you see that movie on TV last night?" The whole family did one peculiar thing I knew about. The way other families went to church, the Sampsons could be found every Labor Day, all day, in front of their TV, to watch the whole of Jerry Lewis's annual muscular dystrophy telethon. Trevor could have no guests on those days, and he could go no farther than the front porch, which is where he and I stood talking one Labor Day when, at one point, his mother stuck her head out the door; looking at Trevor, with a smile that radiated joy, and yet a quiet joy, suggesting humility before the inscrutable mysteries of goodness, she said, "They got twenty-one meelion."

Trevor and I went to different junior high schools and didn't always see much of each other during the school year. But summer had come, and after what I remember as a solid two weeks of dreaming that I was still at Kelly Miller—the way I imagine ex-cons dream that they're still in the joint, soldiers that they're still at war—I realized I was free. From sunup to sundown, while my mother slept before her work shift and my grandmother alternately watched soaps and looked out the window, my only responsibility was to show up at home once in a while and feed myself. The rest of the time? I read my beloved superhero comic books and made up and drew my own. Trevor, with the tact common among us thirteen-year-olds, once told someone in my presence, "Soon, Cliff draw some terrible comics. But he keep tryin', though." I also rode my skateboard, so comfortable on it that I could read comic books at the same time.

And I hung out with Trevor. One day, outside, he spotted a girl who was new to the neighborhood and wanted to talk to her. I went with him. I have retained next to nothing about the girl. I mainly remember Trevor, who was leaning forward with his forearm across one thigh, so he must have had one foot on a front step of the house where the girl was sitting; and what he said interested me. In that time and place, there was much discussion of "talking to" girls— i.e., saying what was necessary to get to the next step. (What you said was your "rap.") I had no idea, none, of how this was done. I thought about girls a lot, but that was all I did. To me, getting some-where with a girl was like standing in front of an enormous building complex and trying to locate, with no information, the room that had what you wanted. You could try to enter the complex and wan-der the halls, but you would look suspicious, and anything seemed better than that. All I knew to do was stand outside and gawk.

And so, when Trevor began "talking to" this girl, I was all ears, but what I heard told me nothing. While I stood just behind him, Trevor asked the girl her name, told her his; asked her how long she had lived here, where she'd been before that; asked her what school she would be going to, what grade she was in, et cetera. At some point the girl's eyes moved from Trevor to me; I moved closer to Trevor, as if for protection. Another question or two, and Trevor said, "See you later," and we walked away. The connection between the conversation I had just heard and having a girlfriend was like the connection between a roomful of guys with computers on Earth and a rocket landing on the moon: I could not make it out. The mystery of talking to girls remained a mystery.

The timing of my joining Boy Scouts of America's Troop 77 was such that I now wonder what was behind it. When my father died, in November 1974—I was eleven—my three friends in Lincoln Heights, the low-income housing project behind my house, already belonged to the troop. Shortly afterward, at their urging, I started going with them to the weekly meetings, held in the basement of a Lutheran church in our neighborhood. Had their mothers whispered to them that they should ask their suddenly fatherless friend along? (My friends, for various reasons, were fatherless themselves, which had a lot to do with why they lived in Lincoln Heights.) Our scoutmaster, the friendly, no-nonsense Mr. Moses, was a young Black man with glasses and a mustache, a wife and toddler, and a surprising amount of gray hair—"from marriage and Vietnam," he told us once. Not counting the many boys who came to a meeting or two and then were never seen again (Trevor was one of those), about a baker's dozen of us could be counted on to show up every week.

Troop 77 had been on camping trips before—I remember pitching tents in the cold dark, my fingers frozen in place like my old GI Joe's well into the next day—but in August 1976 we went to Boy Scout camp. Instead of being on our own deep in the Maryland woods, separated from the elements only by nylon tent walls, sleeping bags, and Mr. Moses's tough love, we were among other troops, all of them white, as were the Boy Scouts of America administrators in charge of us. Mr. Moses didn't go, which had something to do with the way things turned out.

Our troop got split into two campsites of six boys each. We slept two to a tent. My tentmate was Chris, who was nearly as light-skinned as Anthony Wilson. Chris was bigger than me—everybody was—lean and well-muscled like an athlete; I have a memory, like a movie still, of Chris bare-chested, chopping wood. I liked Chris, or I like the memory I have of him, because it is possible that I'm projecting backward, and I understand now, if I didn't then, the difference between gruffness and playfulness on the one hand and meanness on the other. I knew some mean boys when I was thirteen, but Chris was not one of them, not even when he said to me—an allusion to the fact that we in this campsite called ourselves the Bears—"You ain't no bear. You a cub." When he asked about one of the merit badges on the sleeve of my uniform, and I told him it was for "scholastic stuff," he said, "Aw, you punk." But it was Chris who, during long days when the six of us sat around the campsite like soldiers waiting to be sent to the front—and I will come to why we were doing that—it was Chris who came to where I was sitting in the tent reading a comic book and said to me gently, like a parent, "Why don't you come out and hang out for a while?"

"Don't make him put down that comic book," said Little Darryl Silver, one of my Lincoln Heights friends. "That's his life."

He was telling the truth. To the extent that I was connected to life, to the world, superhero comics formed one of the few, thin but strong threads. That had been particularly true since the previous summer, when I read *Origins of Marvel Comics* by Stan Lee, detailing the creation of my favorite costumed heroes—Spider-Man, the Fantastic Four—and the human fears and insecurities they felt behind their masks. I felt I was them, without their masks or powers. And the world contained between the covers of those thin books was filled to bursting, overflowing, with the most wonderful words. (A couple of years later, when I used a word I'd learned from Marvel—"pummel"—in one of my own stories, one of my sisters, a graduate student, said she'd never heard it before.) There were the words the characters spoke, but even better were those in the narration at the tops of the panels, those wonderful, em-dash- and ellipsis-filled musings that helped make sense of what I was seeing. ("Faster than mortal mind can comprehend . . . faster than the *speed of thought* itself . . . two gallant figures pierce the fabric of *infinity* as they hurtle toward . . .") When I wasn't reading Marvel comics, I was trying to create Marvel-like characters of my own. I had, to put it generously, a long way to go, but how I enjoyed the process, the struggle to get the drawings right, or what I thought was right, the joy of having the time, as I didn't in my regular life, to think of what to say.

If I had a favorite Marvel hero, it was probably the Silver Surfer, the gleaming bald alien who was trapped on Earth and both deplored and failed to understand human violence. He rode the skies on a surfboard, which was a little like my skateboard. He hated a fight, the Silver Surfer did, but if you picked one with him, you'd know you were in it. Oh, to be the Silver Surfer . . .

But about the reason we were just hanging out at the campsite:

On our first evening there, looking around that slightly slanted, grass- and dirt- and rock-covered clearing surrounded by trees, I took it upon myself to dispose of food waste left by whichever scouts had stayed there before us. I found what I thought was a good spot, amid some trees a little ways outside the clearing, and dumped it—not knowing what I was letting us all in for. A day or so later, some senior scouts came by our site to check on us, and this was when our single friendly interaction with others took place. One of the senior scouts was a pimply-faced sixteen-year-old whose name I have forgotten. Let's call him Jake. He and Chris, who was the strongest guy in our campsite, had a competition to see who could pump our heavy iron cooking grill over his head the greater number of times. I don't remember who won. I do remember that later that day, or the next day, some adult administrators came to inspect our site. Jake was with them. They nailed us for two infractions. One was that the food waste was too close to the site. Other guys in our troop, who apparently had not seen me dispose of the food, said it had to have been put there by the previous occupants. I said nothing. The other infraction was that the grill was on the ground and not on the stone stove, where it belonged. Jake said nothing. For those two things we were confined to our campsite. (After the administrators left, there was talk among us, although not from me, of catching Jake alone and teaching him a lesson. No doubt fortunately for us, nothing came of that.) And here, I suppose, was my first experience—I don't expect ever to say I've had my last—with the unprovable suspicion that plagues every single Black American. Would a white troop have been grounded for these infractions, or was our punishment a way to avoid dealing with half a dozen Black boys? Here, too, was possibly my first experience with those racially charged situations, always different and always the same, in which the truth manages to be elusive for a few and clear as summer rain for many others. In this case, at least two people knew important things they chose not to say, or felt unable to say, or couldn't find the words for; and I suspect it is that way much of the time.

3. FALL

Dana West was Troop 77's senior patrol leader—the head scout. He was the oldest of my Lincoln Heights friends; the October that I was thirteen, he turned sixteen. The best thing you could call somebody, in that time and place, was "bad." Dana—handsome, lanky, on the light side, short brown hair—was bad. He had sex with girls, or said he did. ("I'm tired of bustin' virgins," he told me one time. I barely knew what he was talking about.) He knew how to fight, standing toe-to-toe with Mr. Moses when the two of them horsed around, even getting the better of him a couple of times, pouring on punches with those big fists of his while Mr. Moses turned his face sideways and covered it, laughing in amazement, "*Hoooooo...*"

And Dana tried to teach me to fight. Why he did is one of the great mysteries of my life. Or maybe the mystery is why I wonder. Why shouldn't Dana have cared enough about me to want to spend his time teaching me self-defense? I've been told a number of times in my life that I am hard to get to know, and I wonder if the reason is that I don't know why anyone would want to know me—I've never been much of a talker, for example—and I have an unease with people who make the effort, an unease stemming from distrust, especially if they seem different from or more interesting than me.

Dana, in some ways, was as different from me as it was possible to be, and yet I not only liked but trusted him, I think because I sensed one way that we were alike. There was a questing in him, a longing for an unnamable something that transcended his surroundings. And I think he sensed, because of my gentleness, detachment, and reputation for book smarts, that I held a key to that mysterious something. Dana would hang out in my basement or my backyard and unspool great stretches of talk, not knowing the meanings of all the words he used or even, some of the time, what he was talking about: observations about girls and boys, his very large family, assessments of our mutual friends based on their Zodiac signs, pronouncements about Blacks and whites. "I'ma tell you, boy," he would start out, and he would tell me a story—"I was walking downtown, and I seen these Africans get out a limousine, they was wearing white robes and head dresses and their skin was so smooth and *black*, man, and *beautiful*, it *glowed* it was so black . . ." Some of what Dana said seems, in retrospect, like undigested chunks of philosophy and theories of history that came from Elijah Muhammad by way of Malcolm X and were disseminated far and wide to eager hearers, including a man Dana spent a lot of time with.

His name was Kenny. I don't know how old he was; he may have been thirty or forty-four. I don't know what he did for a living—the things you don't think to ask, or even wonder, when you're thirteen! I do know that he kept a lot of boys around him, a dozen or so of them present the one time I went with Dana to Kenny's apartment, about a twenty-minute walk in the autumn air from my house. There was talking and joking, there were games of dominoes and demonstrations of form in kung fu, a version of which was the main thing Kenny passed on to his young disciples.

And that is what Dana passed on to me in my basement. We would stand facing each other; he would aim one fist at me while the other returned, in rhythm, to his hip; and my arms, making circles in the air, would block his punches. Then we switched off. What a beating my forearms, those unmuscled sticks, took during those sessions. It didn't matter if I was blocking punches or throwing them—sixty or seventy times per minute my arms collided with Dana's, which were like heavily veined baseball bats. He told me not to massage my arms afterward or shake off the pain: "Absorb it. It makes you stronger." We practiced kicks; we practiced the alphabet, each letter a bodily position, one flowing into the next. Where was all this heading? To the point where, according to Dana, people would see me fight off somebody stupid enough to pick on me and say to themselves, "That nigger *know* some'm."

I struggle, now, to describe the effect all of this had on me. I would love to tell you about an instance when a bully from the previous year tried to pick on the new, Dana-trained me and found himself on the floor, dazed, with the imprint of my tan loafer on his cheek—but I would be writing fiction. The truth is that other boys, all of them bigger than me, would still casually pick on me. Once, in the hallway, a beefy kid named Ricardo thought it would be funny to bring his big blue three-ring notebook, thicker than the Yellow Pages and harder, down on the back of my head. I turned around and punched him in the stomach and chest as he laughed; I might as well have been hitting the side of the Chrysler Building. But I *did* hit back, and maybe, if there was an outer difference in me, that was it. Another time, a guy I was friendly with reached toward me, playfully, to take something of mine; to his surprise, and mine too, my foot knocked away his wrist. And my foot, defining its small, tight arc in the air, may have defined the parameters of the change in me. The world did not look at me and say to itself, "That nigger *know* some'm." I don't even know if *I* thought I knew anything. But there was *something* going on, even if only I could see it, even if I didn't have the words for it.

Whatever it was, I hadn't become a fighter. Once, on a sunny day when we were outside during a Boy Scout meeting, on the sloping lawn of the church where we met, a very stupid kid named Brian did something—I don't remember what, and I'm not sure I even knew at the time—that annoyed Dana. Dana told me to beat him up: "Take care of my light work" was how he put it. I didn't refuse, but neither did I do it. Later, at my house, Dana told me in an even tone that I had shown "too much soft-heartedness." I didn't argue, but neither did I think he was right. Assuming I could have beat Brian up, I saw no reason to.

That didn't prevent a graduation of sorts, a kind of ceremony in my basement that involved Dana's using the words "by the power vested in me" and presenting me with a gold-colored medallion—it showed two guys fighting—and giving me, for reasons I wish I had thought to ask about, a new name: Ming Yang Fu.

When I told my mother that, she tried to stifle her laughter.

4. BIRTHDAY

The irony, I suppose, is that one of the strongest threads connecting me to the world in those days, superhero comics, were so much about fighting. My favorite heroes—Thor, Spider-Man, the Silver

Surfer—fought supervillains as well as one another. It would be easy to say, from the distance of forty-odd years, that those fights were metaphorical, that they were stand-ins for the difficulties of life, and that I saw them in that light even then; it would be easy, but a lie. I *liked* the fights. They were part of the excitement. But I can say that the fights were not nearly all that attracted me. There were the human failings of the characters, and there was also the power—it seemed powerful to me, as I was then—of Stan Lee's writing. And there was the other irony. The words that so often failed me in my daily life—failed me with girls, with friends, with my own mother, in situations in which silence equaled dishonesty—these words made up so much of what I embraced in comics.

That year I had an English teacher who gave us a list of vocabulary words. One of them was "mark." Her example of its usage: "It is not polite to mark the way people talk." When I said to her privately, "Isn't it 'mock'?" she said, "It's both." ("That is *so wrong*," one of my sisters said when I told her.) But my teacher was on the ball in other ways—one, anyhow. She assigned us *The Catcher in the Rye* and, unbeknownst to her, and for a long time unbeknownst to me, changed my world.

Here is where I was with my understanding of novels: I didn't get why Holden Caulfield was the name of the person speaking to me in a real voice—so real that I assumed he was an actual person—when the name on the cover was J. D. Salinger. I read the book slowly, oh so slowly, enraptured. That solid purple cover with the yellow lettering: I sat with it nights at the counter in our tiny kitchen, after my mother had left for work and my grandmother had gone to bed; I read it in the tiny yellow bedroom where I opened this essay, the view of the A-frame across the street now dark and peaceful.

My birthday approached, my fourteenth. This was the one that, by unspoken agreement in our neighborhood, made you somebody. When I was eleven and Dana turned fourteen, he'd said to me in wonder, as if a song he'd written had gone to number one on the Billboard chart, "I'm fourteen, Cliff." The previous year, when my friend Big Darryl Greenfield was acting superior, Little Darryl said, "That sweet fo'teen went to his head." I wanted to finish *Catcher* before I turned fourteen, ahead of my class's schedule, so I stayed up the night before my birthday until I did. There, talking to me in my bedroom, was a Marvel superhero without the superpowers, who said that he couldn't get into fights because he couldn't stand the thought of his fist in the other guy's face, whose story, it became clear as the last page approached, was not going to end in any way I was used to thinking of endings. Here were words without fights, or words that replaced fights, words that could be for me what fighting was in our neighborhood: a way of being in the world.

The next day, fourteen years old, after breakfast with Ma and Grandma, I went to school and told some kids, as they took their seats in the chair-desks in my English class, that I had finished reading the book. Not believing me, they asked me to prove it by telling them the last line. I recited, "Don't ever tell anybody anything. If you do, you start missing everybody." They looked at me, not knowing what to say.

Jazz June

When I was fourteen and nearing the end of eighth grade I developed my first serious crush. The girl, named June, was in ninth grade and about to graduate from Kelly Miller, the junior high school we attended. Given where my crush ultimately got me—i.e., nowhere—June's impending departure, a source of grief for me at the time, was unimportant. June herself, actually, was unimportant. I mean that as a comment not on her worth as a person but on her being the object of my affection, which seems, when I think back on it, almost completely arbitrary. I was of an age and inclination to make one person the center of my can't-sleep-at-night, can't-focus-on-my-homework longing; along came June, hardly gorgeous but pretty enough, nice if not preternaturally sweet. She fit the bill. I had all I needed to be miserable, which I quickly became, not admitting to myself, possibly not even understanding, that my crush was its own point.

June played the violin. I never heard any of her performances myself, but I heard a lot about them. My friend Big Darryl, also a ninth grader, said about a musical number June played at their graduation, "I don't usually like the violin, but she was tearin' it up." I borrowed Darryl's yearbook so that (I didn't tell him this) I could gaze upon and occasionally kiss June's picture, which showed her smiling in her graduation cap. June was part of a group of musical friends to which I was connected tangentially. To have a stronger tie to those superior beings, I signed up that spring of 1977 for summer clarinet lessons with the D.C. Youth Orchestra Program—not to be confused with the actual D.C. Youth Orchestra, the program's elite, of whom June was one. The program had three levels of bands and orchestras, and I got the unspoken message that the orchestras, with their stringed instruments, were considered more important. While I spent that typically sweltering D.C. summer riding two buses to my lessons, squawking and squeaking through quarter and eighth notes, June went away to a music camp, adding physical distance to the other forms of distance separating us. And as I waited that summer for the promised postcard from her, which never arrived, June—and, by association, the violin—came to represent for me an unattainable ideal.

June itself, not the girl but the month, has something about it of the unattainable, the unfulfilled promise. That is, paradoxically, because June, at least in the cities where I have spent my life, is the only reliably spring-like month. Spring officially arrives in late March, finding a lot of people still wearing their winter coats; April and even early May sometimes carry a chill. But in June we can venture outside, where green leaves and flowers are, contending neither with the cold nor with the heat of that long march from Independence Day to Labor Day, that season of commuting in sweat-dampened shirt collars over gradually shortening days. June brings freedom and those wonderful extra hours of sunlight, June whispers that anything is possible, and therein lies the ache: as its days fly by—it is, in the end, just another month, and one of the shorter months at that—we may feel a vague regret over what we have yet again failed to achieve, a hint of sadness for what was promised but not delivered.

There is an answer for this, one that has something in common with my long-ago crush on the girl June: a focus on the feeling itself rather than on where it might lead. In my adopted home, New York City, one way that I revel in the feeling of June, of spring, is to walk across the Brooklyn or Williamsburg Bridge, particularly at night, when the Manhattan skyline is lit, each of the many brightened windows in those tall, tall buildings suggesting industry, energy, creativity. The sense of possibility this inspires, the belief that we can *do*, that we can at least try, may lead somewhere, but it is also a wonderful thing all by itself.

Among her many other poems, the African American writer Gwendolyn Brooks wrote "We Real Cool," perhaps her most famous work. The poem adopts the viewpoint of marginalized Black boys who shoot pool together. Brooks explained about the passage "We / Jazz June" that these boys, effectively locked out of mainstream society, gleefully attack its cherished symbols: to June, that month of wedding announcements in newspapers' society pages, the boys bring jazz, originally the music of the low-down. ("Jazz" was once a verb, synonymous with "fuck.")

I may have read that explanation in a textbook, but it's possible—and this is the version of events I prefer—that I heard it from Brooks's own lips, on the one, cringe-worthy occasion when I met her. This was in New York in 1991. I was a freelance (read: unemployed) writer of twenty-eight, scrounging for a living, and I had signed on to write a young adult biography of Brooks. In ninety-nine cases out of a hundred, such books are cobbled together with information from secondary sources, but I saw in the newspaper that Brooks was giving a reading in Manhattan, and so I went, hoping to infuse my project with insights that only the poet herself could provide. To my delight, one of the poems she read that night was "We Real Cool." After the reading, while Brooks greeted friends and signed books, I lurked late, waiting for my chance to speak to her. Finally, noticing this silent young stranger, she turned to me, curious. I explained what I was doing, and she asked what she could do for me. And then, God help me, I said to this Pulitzer

Prize–winning septuagenarian, "I was hoping I could buy you a cup of something."

I should say here, to portray Brooks in an appropriately positive light and make myself look like less of a fool, that she later personally mailed me materials she thought would help my project. In that moment, though, maybe misinterpreting my offer—or, possibly worse, understanding it perfectly—she bent double with laughter, long, loud laughter of embarrassment for me, for us. It's probably superfluous to report that I bought the poet no cups of anything that night, or ever. As she laughed I felt sorry I had said what I did, sorry I'd come at all to see this woman, who seemed to have about as much use for me as did my old schoolmate June.

We / Jazz June. I have another way of observing and celebrating June: I listen to the late Jaki Byard's solo piano jazz record *Blues for Smoke*, recorded in 1960. Whatever the reason, and it may well be purely subjective, the tunes on *Blues for Smoke*, none more so than "Spanish Tinge No. 1," make me think of soft June nights, of walking slowly, perhaps aimlessly, through dark streets lined with trees that are thick with leaves, the yellow glow of the occasional street lamp illuminating just enough green foliage to hint at its black depths.

There is also the six-minute title track of Sonny Rollins's album *The Bridge*, from 1962. Prior to making that album, Rollins, a young turk of the tenor saxophone, had found himself being praised by jazz critics even as he sometimes failed to play as well as he wanted. To bring himself closer to what he felt he could do, to pursue what he hoped was possible, Rollins stopped performing and recording for a time and took to practicing his horn on the Williamsburg Bridge. "The Bridge," a nod to those days and nights of dogged self-improvement, features contrasts. Rollins plays in a rapid tempo that occasionally slows, possibly reflecting the ebb and flow of traffic on the bridge; and while he often races up and down chords, seemingly playing every note in existence, he sometimes plays impressionistically, blowing isolated two- or four-note phrases, dabs of sound, bringing to mind the pinpoints of light from office windows of the Manhattan skyline. Rollins's practice sessions were not recorded. Still, sometimes during those June walks over the Williamsburg Bridge, I think of those no doubt beautiful sounds, those expressions of feeling, played not long before my birth and heard mainly by Rollins himself. I am happy to be where that music was made, even if it can't be heard, even if, in the traditional sense, it got nowhere.

I own a clarinet—not the one I had as a teen but one given to me years later by a friend who found it in the apartment she had just moved into and remembered that I had once played. I don't play anymore. Truth is, I was never very good. There are a number of possible explanations for that—an obvious one, which I don't discount, is simple lack of talent—but an important one may be that I didn't have a model. At age fourteen I didn't know from jazz and wouldn't for years, and so I was without a sense of what was possible on the instrument.

That is not a real regret. I am more than content, today, to be a fan, and to subject my wife and daughters to my fandom. They are good-natured about it. On a recent, chilly autumn day I pulled out one of my oldest jazz CDs, a compilation of the work of the alto saxophonist Julian "Cannonball" Adderley, and played it for my teenaged younger daughter. I have long maintained that the late Cannonball possessed the sweetest sound in all of jazz; I drew my daughter's attention in particular to a ballad called "Spring Is Here," a work my wife once pronounced to be "too beautiful." As we listened to that indeed almost inexpressibly lovely tune, I realized something that I hadn't during the innumerable times I had played this record before, and I said to my daughter about Cannonball's delicate, quivering tone, "He made his horn sound like a violin." And even as, outside, the fall wind stirred brown leaves and deposited them in piles on the wide sidewalks of our Brooklyn neighborhood, I thought for just a moment, hearing that sweet jazz, of June.

On the Bus

ON THE GIRLS OF YOUTH,
TRAVEL, TV, WRITING,
AND CRITICISM

1. 1979

I was sixteen, standing among adults in a parking lot on a morning in late summer. One of the adults was my cousin Billy Thompson. "Sorry about that," he said to me, looking around at the cars and the forty or so other Black folks in the lot. He used the word "sorry" the way my whole family and I do, the way that tends to confuse people, since we are not accepting blame for your misfortune, just expressing sympathy. Billy was sorry that from the look of things, no one else my age was coming on this bus trip to New Orleans. No doubt I shrugged and gave the other family line—"Oh, well"—which was meant to disguise what I was thinking: No other kids on this trip? No strangers I'll be expected to interact with, whether or not we have anything in common, which, given my solitary and fairly odd nature, we most likely don't? What's to be sorry about?

I went on these weeklong bus trips with my mother, varying combinations of our relatives, and assorted strangers for three consecutive summers. This was the second. The bus/hotel package deals were the kind of thing my mother could afford now. Her nights at the post office brought her a good salary by the standards of our neighborhood; more to the point—and unbeknownst to me—her life had become easier, financially speaking, with my father's death five years earlier, because now he couldn't gamble away her paycheck. My mother, probably for the first time in her adult life, didn't have to worry about money. The bus trips were a way of finally enjoying herself a little. Beyond providing for her family, my mother, the most practical of people, had never wanted much, and her pleasures had been the simplest ones: a glass of scotch here, a can of Miller High Life there, a good laugh. If I started to tell my mother something funny, she would laugh a little in joyful anticipation, rocking quietly, before I even got to the funny part, as if revving the engine of her mirth. With dentures to replace the rotted teeth of my earliest memories, she could now laugh without putting her hand in front of her mouth. My mother had her dark moods too, times when she felt overburdened and underappreciated. "Don't make no kinda effort to do *nothin*!" she once told me about my house-cleaning habits, a statement that is branded on my memory. But those moods were occasional and reserved for family; they never surfaced, for example, during the bus trips.

I say "bus trips," but "bus vacations" may be more like it. With the destinations so far from Washington—New Orleans this year, Disney World the previous year, Chicago the next—no small part of our time was spent just getting to those places and back, always passing one night at a motel along the way, in a nondescript town in the Carolinas, say. And so a lot of the social scene took place on the bus: talking, laughing, playing cards. During the trip to Florida, the scene had included a pair of teenage sisters, one a chubby, retiring girl whose name and exact age I don't recall, the other sixteen-year-old Tawana, light-skinned but dark-featured like an Italian, pregnant but not showing yet. Tawana liked talking to me, for reasons I didn't understand, since her life experience—which gave her the jaded air of a divorced forty-year-old—made mine seem nonexistent, which it pretty much was. On the other hand, since I was unable to match her stories, I made for a good, sympathetic listener, easy for her to talk to about her past boyfriends and such.

For several weeks after our return from Florida, Tawana would call me on the phone nearly every day, invariably responding to my "Hello?" with "You busy?" That she might have desired more than friendship with an innocent like me was so ridiculous that it didn't cross my mind; a third of a century later, I wonder. My roommate on the Florida trip was a twelve-year-old boy, Mike, who was related to me—or wasn't—in that unclear way of large Black families originating in small southern towns. Mike was built like a small tank, while I, three years older and taller, looked like a stick by comparison. (That word comes to mind because of what Tawana said about me: "Cliff ain't nothin but a stick noway." I forget the context.) Rounding out the group of young people was Mary, at fourteen a year younger than me. Mary was skinny with medium-brown skin and chewed-up nails and was neither ugly nor pretty. She could not have been more different from me. I was the kind of introspective kid who got good grades but could get lost in his own neighborhood. I used words like "sarcastic." Once, for example, I said something to Mary that she didn't understand, then explained that I was being sarcastic. She said, "How can you tell if a star-castic person is talking straight?" Mary's intelligence, unlike mine, was directed entirely outward, toward getting the things she wanted—one of those being me. Alone with me in my hotel room one evening, she feigned fright at the thunder outside, came to where I was sitting, and got in my lap. I didn't protest, and she gave me my first kiss.

But all of that was last year.

This year, as the closest thing to a kid on this trip, I was free to just think my thoughts, to be quiet until I had something to say—to be myself, in other words. My roommate was Billy, who had said he was sorry there was no one else my age with us: Billy, a bachelor of thirty-five, beefy and very dark-skinned with a medium-length Afro and black-framed glasses of the kind they don't make anymore, the lenses so thick they looked like skim milk; Billy the elementary school teacher, irrepressible talker, and inveterate joker, Billy who lived with his mother (my aunt Bessie, also on this trip) and had things whispered about him. I really liked him. Seeing me do things like make ridiculous faces as I swan-dived into the hotel bed we shared, he told me, "You're as full of humor as I am." I took that as a great compliment, considering some of the things he said and did. One night he talked in his sleep—or so I thought—complaining loudly about others on the trip while I said "Billy! Billy, wake up!" until he gave himself away, bursting into that great laugh of his. Billy's pièce de résistance, at least on that trip, came during a rest stop in Alabama. Someone on that bus full of Black people bought a local newspaper, which contained a quarter-page ad for a Ku Klux Klan rally. Billy, meanwhile, got off the bus carrying the covering he put over himself while napping; getting back on board with whatever snack he had bought, he put the white sheet over his head like a Klansman, to howls of nervous laughter from everyone else.

We stayed in the French Quarter, taking tours during the day. It may have been during one of these that Billy spotted a white boy of about thirteen who he swore had been in *Americathon*, a now-forgotten movie he had just seen; I guess he was right, since the boy agreed to give Billy an autograph. In the main I remember two things about New Orleans: eating a great deal of very good food and walking at night down the middle of Bourbon Street, past a lot of wild-looking places I wasn't old enough to enter. At one of them a mustached white man in a cowboy hat and cowboy boots stood in the entrance, repeatedly kicking the wooden swing door open to give glimpses of the women dancing inside. Safely ensconced in a group of adults, in no danger of being taken seriously, I feigned irritation at being barred from these places—never mind that I wouldn't have known the first thing to do if someone had let me in. Before one evening stroll I borrowed somebody's mascara brush and painted a mustache on myself, pretending to think this would get me into someplace. Most of the adults laughed; a couple looked annoyed.

Human beings are peculiar animals, and just as the average income in a neighborhood can be a figure that matches no one's salary, the hidden details of our lives, if laid bare, would leave very, very few of us—I am convinced of this—looking what we call "normal."

My happiest moment of our New Orleans vacation came about not in that storied city but en route there, during a time when I was, you may not be surprised to learn, alone. It was late, past midnight, and we were on the bus. I had two seats to myself, and everyone else was asleep, or seemed to be. Quiet reigned. The only sound was the rush of the bus down the highway, the only things visible the lights from the small number of cars and trucks in front of us—those, and the book in my lap, illuminated by the narrow ray of the overhead light.

The book, which my older brother had brought along, was Tim Brooks and Earle Marsh's *The Complete Directory to Prime Time TV Shows, 1946–Present*. Here were articles, ranging from a paragraph to a page or two, about every evening television show I had ever watched—and baby, I had watched a lot of them—plus many, many more I hadn't seen or even heard of. Here were *Gilligan's Island*, *M*A*S*H*, *The Mary Tyler Moore Show*, *Good Times*, and all the other programs I had actively viewed or had on in the background while I did my homework or played with my toys; here were the sources of those flickering blue images (these were the last days of black-and-white TV) that infused the atmosphere of our house like dust mites, like the air itself. The articles recounted the shows' premises, described the characters, and, in many cases, gave critical analyses. Reading the analyses was like looking down from a helicopter at the street where I'd lived my whole life, seeing utterly familiar things from a brand-new angle. In the entry about *Sanford and Son*, the sitcom about a cantankerous, ailing, sixty-five-year-old junk dealer and his resentful, complaining thirty-year-old son and caretaker, I read that the son, Lamont—I am quoting all this from memory—"would never have left the old man." No, come to think of it, I guess he wouldn't have! "Although it was never thrown out at the audience," I read about the warm, attractive, single main character of *The Mary Tyler Moore Show*, Mary Richards "could spend the night with a man she wasn't in love with." I had never thought to put it that way, but yes, that was probably right! The seven marooned individuals on *Gilligan's Island* never made it back to civilization, which "was perhaps unfortunate, as this exceedingly simple-minded farce might have ended much sooner if [Gilligan] had found a way back." *Exceedingly simple-minded*—ha ha, yes! I even enjoyed reading about shows I'd never seen. One, on which real, ordinary people told the audience about funny incidents in their lives, "seemed like a good idea for television in 1948," the entry drily and knowingly concluded.

Reading this book was pure pleasure. If someone had asked me why I was enjoying it so much, I would have said simply, "It's a lot of fun to read about shows I've been watching my whole life." But in retrospect, I think it may have been my first experience of a writer's leading me, in a way I could understand, beneath the surface of things—and then stepping outside those things to show them for what they were. I would not have used the word "criticism," but this was the first exposure to it I can remember.

I read until my eyes began to close, and then I turned out the overhead light, joining the others on the bus in darkness. The bus rolled on; we moved toward our destination, and I, like many young people who live in their own heads, had a sense of a larger, grander destination beyond that one, a place at which my arrival was all but assured, because I was smart, because I was creative, because I had so many years to get there.

2. 2013

Another moment in the dark: early December, the end of the year creeping near, not the object of immediate attention but visible in the distance. I was fifty years old. At around four in the morning I lay in the dark next to my wife, who was sound asleep while I, not for the first time recently, or the second, or the third, was unaccountably but completely awake.

One's mind in these circumstances—mine, at least—is the way I picture outer space: a black, orderless non-place where thoughts, like comets or debris or light from dying stars, crisscross and collide. No beginning, no end. One point as good as another. Let's see:

To my relief and my anguish, the days of playing on the floor with our two daughters, of making up bedtime stories to tell them every night and sitting next to them while they went to sleep, were behind me. One daughter was fifteen, bright and funny and just as introverted as her old man—and, come to think of it, the exact age I was on that first bus trip, a year older than Mary (she of my first kiss) had been at the time, nearly as old as the worldly, lonely, pregnant Tawana. (What was Tawana doing now? Or her baby, now thirty-four?) Our other daughter was now twenty, this grown person who was somehow my child, who liked jazz and hip-hop and Johnny Cash, who read Hemingway, who aspired to be—of all the things the daughter of an introvert could try to become—an actor. Had I done a good job by them? All I could say for sure was that I had tried as the years slipped by, and that the job, done well or badly, was just about done.

I was just about done, too, emotionally if not otherwise, with another job: the editing career that had fed us while, in my off-hours, I wrote, and wrote, and wrote. Writing was the route I had chosen to the destination I imagined so long ago. It had led me through miles, and years, of wilderness, a no-man's-land whose ends I had finally reached, or not. My recently published book of essays, much of it criticism, had appeared to an explosion of quiet—and then, miraculously, caught the eye of an award committee, and so transformed me from an aging, highly obscure writer into an aging, highly obscure writer with a prize. I was pleased and grateful for this award, given to those who show "promise" (promise!), but I wasn't sure what, at this stage, that meant, or even what this stage was, or what was next, which was true of my life generally at this moment, that possibly being one reason why, at four-something in the morning, I was wide awake.

In the dark I thought of other things, too, many and small and random: grievances now two decades old that I should have long forgotten, things I wished I'd said back to this or that person, sex, snatches of old TV shows . . . I wondered sometimes what effect TV had had on me, on us all. Things had changed a bit lately, but in general, through TV's history, life had tended to go well for its characters, provided they were decent folks, and didn't most of us think of ourselves as decent folks? What unconscious assumptions had we all taken from this? How many of us, because of TV, had spent our lives waiting on things that would never come? Was I among them? Well, hey, at least my formative years had coincided with seventies TV, which had little touches of reality: Mary Richards of *The Mary Tyler Moore Show* never did find Mr. Right—didn't marry him, anyway. The dad on *Good Times* died, and so did poor Henry Blake on *M*A*S*H*, on his way home from the Korean War.

And, of course, for evidence of things not working out as they should, one need not look to TV. After my grandmother died, my mother got to enjoy some freedom—which lasted five short years before her own decline began, culminating in her death two years later. Then there was Billy, who at age sixty, still single, overweight and with high blood sugar, stepped out of his bathroom one day and apparently sank from a standing position, sliding down the wall to the crouch in which he died. I thought of seeing Billy at a relative's funeral in 1987, eight years after our time in New Orleans; we had reminisced about the trip, and then he pulled out his wallet, fat as a brick with photos and God knows what else, and retrieved from among innumerable slips of paper the one with the autograph from the young *Americathon* actor. That gesture made me sad even then. For what, for whom, did my funny, gifted cousin carry around this forgotten performer's immature scrawl? What was the point?

That question, applied in most unoriginal fashion to the rest of life, was also on my mind at 4:00 a.m. During those trips in the late 1970s, I had passed the time by playing cards and playing chess as the bus moved on, heading to a place better than where I was. I was still, metaphorically speaking, playing cards and chess, but— ironically, given the late evidence of progress—my faith in the destination, or in the certainty of my arrival, was wavering. Or was my fear that I had already arrived?

Still: on at least one occasion, I had done more on the bus than pass the time. Reading the TV book played its part in the opening of my mind to a new way of looking at the world, of being in it.

I didn't think of things that way at the time, of course. I simply immersed myself in what I was doing, managing to enjoy the ride without worrying too much about where I was going, or how much of the journey was left. And so my sixteen-year-old self had a lesson to pass down through the decades, if only, lying there in the dark, and this is by no means certain, I could hear it.

Cities, Bulls, and the Boy at Seventeen

ON CRITICISM,

ROMANTIC YEARNING,

FILM, AND REDEMPTION

Washington residents of a certain age will remember the late Davey Marlin-Jones. For the evening news broadcast on Channel 9, the local CBS affiliate, Marlin-Jones gave movie reviews, but calling him a film critic is sort of like calling *Macbeth* a story about a married couple: there's a little more to it than that. Marlin-Jones wore wide-brimmed fedoras and three-piece suits, and he looked almost as if he were wearing one of those plastic eyeglasses/big-nose/ handlebar-mustache combos that used to be a staple of kids' birthday parties, but on him the parts were all real. Delivering reviews in an unaffectedly comical voice, he referred to a stack of notecards, one for each movie under discussion. At the end of a review, if he liked the movie, he would place the card in the inside pocket of his jacket; if he didn't, he would toss it, the cue for the studio sound-effects man to make it land with a crash. If Marlin-Jones found a movie to be well worth seeing but flawed, he would tear off a corner of the card—representing his reservations—and put the rest in his pocket, whereas if a movie was abysmal except for, say, one good performance, he would pocket the corner and toss the rest. This showmanship, this eccentricity, was not meant to hide a lack of critical powers. Marlin-Jones gave thoughtful, sharp reviews, criticism so good I still remember parts of it after three decades. He called *Return to Oz* "a movie for people who hate children and aren't too fond of themselves." He once said that Kim Basinger was "not a bad actress. She is a non-actress," and his concluding statement about a movie in which she starred was "*Nine and a Half Weeks*: it only *seems* that long."

Davey Marlin-Jones, as that review will suggest, was not one people suspected of being on movie studios' payroll. A good review from him meant something. And so one broadcast in 1980 got my full attention. At the end of a review, this jaded, acerbic critic held his notecard in both hands, leaned forward, looked straight into the camera, and said in complete earnest, "This is a brilliant—brilliant—film." The film was Martin Scorsese's *Raging Bull*.

I was seventeen that year. They've stopped making seventeen-year-olds of the kind I was—they had mostly stopped making them then—and that is in no way a boast. Today's seventeen-year-olds seem to have lived complete lives already, with résumés barely contained on one page, with not only lovers but ex-lovers. My résumé when I was seventeen would have fit inside a fortune cookie, and as for lovers, there is nothing to discuss. I did have a life—one that took place largely inside my head. I planned to conquer the world through the comics I had been drawing for nearly a decade, not realizing that this ambition was already crumbling. There were girls I liked, and I even called them on the phone, talking to them sometimes for hours about everything except what I wanted to say, circling like a shark around a small island, no more able to come to the point than the shark was able to grow legs and walk up to its prey.

There was one exception to all this living in my head: a girl who was a year behind me in high school. She was—I write this to my shame—too heavy to fit my idea of a girlfriend, but she was not unattractive. She was not exactly shy, either, and she made it clear that she wanted me for a boyfriend. It was equally clear that things weren't quite right with her, though not—this is especially plain in retrospect—the things she claimed. She sometimes got searing, blinding, and completely imaginary headaches because of . . . her brain tumor. When these "headaches" came on, it helped a lot to ease the pain, she suggested, if I kissed her. Did I believe all this? No, at least not completely, and yet I went along with it, kissing and all, in part for reasons I can't explain, in part for reasons that probably need no explanation. The first time this happened, we were in the theater to see the movie Davey Marlin-Jones had sold me on— *Raging Bull*. I ended up missing parts of the movie and not concentrating fully on what I did see. When it was over, I apologized to this girl, saying that I shouldn't have kissed her, because as much as I liked her, I didn't feel "that way." She got *good* and mad.

I wasn't done discovering what a singularly bad date movie *Raging Bull* is. But I'm getting ahead of my story.

This was the fall of 1980, when the days were getting shorter, when the wind in D.C. began to carry a chill and shook brown leaves from trees, when I stood like a skier looking down the length of my final year of high school, not sure what lay at the bottom. College? Yes, but where? I would leave my mother, my grandmother, and my sisters—now returned from their graduate studies—to do . . . what? I had the sense of a big world "out there" for me to discover, which both excited and scared me. I was, if not quite consciously, attuned to things I didn't understand, a category that includes a great deal even now and that in 1980 comprised just about everything. I had read a few books, but only a few. I had always loved movies, finding some funny (*A Day at the Races*, *Uptown Saturday Night*), some exciting (*The 7th Voyage of Sinbad*, *Rocky*), some stirring, partly because of their soundtracks (Motown in *Cooley High*, Simon & Garfunkel songs in *The Graduate*), but what did it mean when a film was "brilliant"? What language was that? That question had driven me to the theater for *Raging Bull*, and though I was distracted while watching it, I thought I had a faint glimmer of understanding. *Raging Bull*, like *Rocky*, is about a boxer, but the resemblance ends there, and not just because the former was shot in black and white, the latter in color. *Rocky* is about believing in yourself enough to pursue a dream, one that goes beyond what you've ever felt capable of; as thrilling as the boxing scenes are, boxing is nearly incidental to the story, which could almost be about running or auto racing. And while winning is supposedly beside the point in *Rocky*—the title character loses, very narrowly, in the end—it really isn't, because the excitement in the film is the direct result of how very close Rocky comes to victory. By contrast, for the real-life Jake LaMotta, as portrayed by Robert De Niro in *Raging Bull*, boxing is not a vehicle but a natural extension of this man's blind, deep-seated aggression. His many wins have the feel of defeat, since he is demonstrating through them the sum total of what he can do as a human being. Many times over the course of the film he raises his arms in victory, but he seems no prouder at those moments than at the end of the savage, nearly unwatchable beating he takes at the hands of his nemesis, Sugar Ray Robinson, whom he taunts with "You never got me down, Ray." *Raging Bull* made *Rocky* look like what it is—a very good cartoon—and suggested that brilliance might lie in showing a subject not as we want it to be but as it actually is.

I think, anyway, that I took this in at seventeen, in that period of my mind's groping. I was, speaking of cartoons, coming toward the end of my drawing, finding it inadequate (or finding my ability to do it inadequate) for what I wanted to express—not that I knew exactly what that was, or what a better mode might be. Full of feeling, clueless about what to do with it, I sometimes went for aimless walks alone in other parts of D.C., going past bookstores and coffee shops near Dupont Circle, passing the townhouses and spindly trees along P Street en route to Georgetown. I found that I liked doing this on Sunday, when the city's weekend craziness (which I had missed, sitting at home) had spent itself and the mellower side of city life was on display: elegantly dressed people eating at outdoor tables, or men in moth-eaten-just-so jackets glimpsed through windows as they read books and nursed cups of coffee. This love of a city seen through a beautifying lens had a counterpart in another black-and-white movie I saw in a second-run theater around this time: Woody Allen's *Manhattan*.

I'd like to be able to write here that I saw those opening shots in *Manhattan* at seventeen and was so struck by their beauty that my love and appreciation for great cinema was born on the spot. The truth is that my eye for purely visual beauty, in film, in painting, took a while to develop—is, I hope, still developing. I saw *Manhattan* again recently; I took in that first sequence, with Woody Allen's comic-wistful voiceover, with the swelling woodwinds and brass of Gershwin's *Rhapsody in Blue*, with, most of all, those black-and-white shots of the city, and my middle-aged jaw, I swear to you, fell. But in 1980, as the cinematography and the references to Dovzhenko's *Earth* and Cezanne's apples went flap-flap over my head, I responded to the film's humor and to the ambiguity of its ending. "You have to have a little faith in people," says Tracy (played by Mariel Hemingway), the film's youngest and most emotionally intelligent character. This, the last line of the movie, left part of me thinking, "Wait, you can't stop *there!*" and another, quieter part sensing that I'd stumbled onto a kind of storytelling I hadn't known about.

I'm not sure if, or how many times, I saw *Manhattan* between my first viewing and the most recent one. Once, maybe? I've seen *Raging Bull* several times over the years, though. I remember one viewing particularly well. It took place in a theater in late 1989, nearly a decade after I'd first seen the movie with my high school friend. This time, too, I went with a young woman, and this time, too, I was distracted from what was happening on the screen, but for very different reasons, and in a way that actually revealed something to me about *Raging Bull*—namely, what an unrelentingly harsh film it is. During the scene when Joey (Joe Pesci) is slamming the head of Salvy (Frank Vincent) with a taxi door, I looked over at my date, who was sunk down in her seat, her face covered with tears. (It seems she forgave me for putting her through that. We have since married and raised two children together.)

I saw *Raging Bull* again recently. It sounds like a joke to say that *Raging Bull* and *Manhattan* take on the same themes—since the latter focuses on the relationship entanglements of a nervous intellectual, the former on the life and career of a brute—but I contend that they do. In addition to their New York setting and gorgeous black-and-white cinematography, the two films have in common the theme of humans' inevitable tendency to hurt one another, intentionally or not. The insecure, neurotic Mary (Diane Keaton), the figure at the center of *Manhattan*'s five-person romantic pileup, is not the film's emotional center; that role belongs to the seventeen-year-old Tracy, who is, perhaps because of her youth, the purest figure in the story—and it is this sweet young person whom the Allen character, for all his moral pronouncements, for all his reluctance to do so, ends up wounding. Jake LaMotta of *Raging Bull*, of course, beats up men for a living—nothing personal—but what he can't beat is his own jealousy; thanks to De Niro's performance, you can all but see the workings of Jake's small brain, see him connecting all the wrong dots, until the resulting violence drives away the only people he cares about. Given that each of us is ultimately out for himself, the center of his own world; given that we will hurt others whether we are the conscientious intellectual or the insanely jealous professional fighter, why even try to do right, to treat others well? Together, the two films suggest an answer: other people, for all their own capacity to hurt, and despite evidence to the contrary, are generally worth it. Witness Jake LaMotta, alone in the world, his career over, trying, however pathetically, to resurrect himself as a performer of the works of Shakespeare and Paddy Chayefsky—trying to become a human being. *You have to have a little faith in people.*

In the spring of 1986 I had an office job in Georgetown. By then I had been to college in Ohio and back; I had been hurt, and I had inflicted some hurt, too, none of it on purpose. And there was more to come: I was about to move, to take another office job, this one in . . . Manhattan.

I was still in Georgetown, though, walking around at lunch one day, when, along with several other people on the sidewalk, I saw a familiar face. Actually, the face was less familiar than the things on and around it: the fedora, the glasses, the handlebar mustache, all of it just like on TV. Seeing my eyes on him, Davey Marlin-Jones smiled at me and said in that same comical voice, "How goes your world?"—not stopping to hear the answer, continuing his journey in a world of his own.

Equinox

ON FILM, WRITING,

AMBITION, AND JAZZ

I was seventeen, alone one summer night in a hotel room in Chicago, sitting on the edge of the bed and flipping channels on the TV, when I happened on it. Coming in during the thick of the action, I had no idea what I was watching—and wouldn't for many years—but I knew I had never seen anything quite so strange. The movie's main characters, a handful of young adults, seemed to be searching for something having to do with the occult—a book was involved—and their search had led them to a wooded area; that was as much of the plot as I could make out. The rest was pure weirdness. Over time, as most of the images faded like steam from my memory, I would retain three: a fistfight between two male friends, the odd grin worn by the winner suggesting that he was possessed; a green, human-like monster, twice the height of a man, knocking down one of the main characters with a lazy swing of its flabby arm; and what I remembered as the final image—one of the characters in a mental hospital, screaming as he's restrained by staff, while a voiceover announces in an ominous bass, "In one year and one day, you will be dead!" Those were the clues in my intermittent efforts, carried out over the next, pre-Google decade and a half, to find out what I had seen, to prove to myself that I *had* seen it, that those cine-fragments were not refugees from some hidden horror chamber in my own mind.

That was not the only mystery in my life at the time. The hotel stay in Chicago, one of the family vacations that included so, so many hours on a bus, took place in August of 1980, near the end of the summer between my junior and senior years of high school, a period of between-ness in a larger way too. The setting and circumstances of my childhood had done their work—this person-forming, memory-making machinery had spat me out, and there I stood, naked, cooling, yet to go forth. Go forth and do what?

There were clues. I had begun reading novels, their wonderful, musty book-smell wafting up to me as I sat late at night at the counter in our little kitchen. As with the movie I had or hadn't seen, the books themselves presented a mystery. Many were modern classics—*A Separate Peace*, *Raise High the Roof Beam, Carpenters*—the definition of "modern classic" seeming to be a novel in which you found yourself wondering, three pages from the end, how the author could possibly wrap things up in the remaining six or seven paragraphs. And usually, in fact, the author *didn't* wrap things up, at least not according to the storytelling conventions I had taken in like air from the beginnings of my consciousness, the tried-and-true beginning/middle/happy ending. With so much left unsaid by the end of these books, I had the dim sense, as I'd never had while reading comic books or, say, Hardy Boys novels, of a ghostly presence *behind* the words on the page—a sense that the words themselves, even the events they described, were secondary, mere clues about the animating spirit at work, one that was as inscrutable as a deity.

From age seventeen, another seventeen years passed. My movements during that intervening time, which felt as I made them like steps across a dark room, had added up in retrospect to a laughably, boringly age-appropriate pattern: the tortured romances, chaotic travel, and professional directionlessness of my twenties had given way in my thirties to marriage, steady employment, and fatherhood, so that I found myself, at age thirty-four, doing the old American two-step—from home to the office, from the office to home—only with less dancing room than usual, since my growing family and I lived in New York City.

But mysteries remained. Toward the end of high school I had set out to understand those deities whose presence I'd sensed, even tried to become one myself. An English major in college and a voracious reader since, I had tried to write novels, with results that might best be compared to attempts at air travel before the Wright brothers—impressive in their way, probably better than most people could do, yet lacking that certain something, as crucial as it was elusive, that would make them take off. Still, as I imagine was true of those would-be pioneers, the frustration was matched by the exhilaration of the attempt, the joy of the creative act and the hope that maybe, maybe, this time . . . All of that kept me going as I wrote in longhand in notebooks during my lunch hours in the company cafeteria and later, when I got one, in my office; all of that drove me as I sat at our living room desktop computer late into Friday nights, after my wife and little daughter had gone to sleep, typing in what I'd written during the week. Was this the way one became, or conjured, a deity?

This was the ongoing mystery—one of them, anyway. There were other, smaller ones, easier to answer. One evening when I was thirty-four, for example, I sat in a coffeehouse with a friend I'd known for several years, a portly, balding, mustached, very amiable guy who was as big a lover of films as I was and had seen even more of them. As I had with several other people over the years, I mentioned to my friend the mysterious movie I had either seen or imagined in Chicago seventeen years earlier; I described how weird it was, how the memory of the little bit I had seen continued to fascinate me.

"And then," I said, "the poor guy is in the hospital screaming, and this voice says, 'In one year and one day, you will be dead!'"

Usually, by this point in my story, my listener was looking at me with concern or else thinking about something else altogether. And so I was surprised when, instead, my friend's eyes lit up in recognition. Snapping his fingers, pointing at me, he said, "*Equinox!*"

The mystery movie now had a name! By this time we had entered the age of the Information Superhighway, and, armed with a title, I read online about this work I had begun to think I'd imagined. I learned about *Equinox*'s very young creators, Dennis Muren (later of special-effects fame), Mark McGee, and David Allen; about the film's $6,500 budget; about how another director, Jack Woods, eventually took over and shot additional scenes to make *Equinox* feature-length; about the cult status the film had earned among horror-film geeks since its 1970 release; and about how Muren, McGee, and Allen had put all their hearts into the project—inspired by those who had come before them, driven by love and hope.

As I wrote during lunch hours in the company cafeteria or in my office, as I typed late into Friday nights, I often listened to jazz records on my headphones, sometimes the work of John Coltrane—who in the fall of 1960 recorded a tune called "Equinox." The tune begins with low, ominous piano notes; then Coltrane, on tenor saxophone, plays the simple theme repeatedly, seeming to mull over the idea of it, each iteration more complex than the one before, until, at last, he takes off, begins to take the theme apart, seeing what it's made of, what he can make out of it, playing faster as he explores, his sound—as it always did—giving the feel of a search, a quest.

That, perhaps, is the quality that Coltrane's fans continue to respond to, decades after his death at age forty: not the dense weave of crisscrossing notes played at light speed, not the intensity (Trane eventually took to playing with two drummers simultaneously, one being insufficient to drive him as he needed to be driven); perhaps they respond, rather, to what they sense *behind* it all, an unseen something that this jazz mystic sought relentlessly even as it seemed to speak through him, to possess him.

From age thirty-four, more years passed—time I spent doing the two-step through promotions, my second daughter's birth, parent-teacher conferences, family vacations, graduations, laughter and tears, and the growth of my jazz collection, all the while trying to summon the spirit that would animate my fiction. A funny thing happened with that. I succeeded—in my own estimation—once, self-publishing the result after the world appeared to disagree; meanwhile, I conjured a different spirit, or it spoke through me. To put it a different way, I started writing essays.

Years pass, with things big and small that we mean to do, some getting done, others, well . . . One of the small things I eventually accomplished was to purchase my very own DVD of *Equinox*, the mysterious film that I glimpsed at seventeen, that I learned the title of at thirty-four, that I finally watched in its entirety at fifty-two.

When you're seventeen, your twenties, thirties, and forties—assuming you think about them—may seem like unknown, mysterious lands to be explored. Moving through them, you come gradually to a realization that challenges an unconscious assumption. As different and new as these lands seem, you will not find in them a new essential self; you continue to feel like you, and if, for that reason, the new lands begin to resemble the ones you've already passed through—if, that is, it begins to seem that there is nothing new ahead—you may arrive at that classic question, *Is this it?*

With luck you work out an answer to that question that you can live with. Meanwhile, you may apply the question to other, smaller matters. *Equinox*, for example, a work I long thought of as offering a peek into the wonderfully dark, weird world of an auteur's imagination, a work I chased down, however lazily, over decades, turns out to be (*is that all?*) a decidedly substandard piece of filmmaking. Much of the acting is eye-poppingly bad; the effects are cheesy—the monsters move like the Abominable Snow Monster in *Rudolph the Red-Nosed Reindeer*; and some parts just plain don't make sense. I watched the movie with my younger daughter, seventeen herself now, who said with a laugh when it was over, "That's the greatest thing I've ever seen!"—meaning that it was not just awful but hilariously, transcendently awful. And yet there is something else going on, too, something oddly compelling about it all.

The story that unfolds in *Equinox* is told to a reporter by Dave (played by Edward Connell) from his bed in the mental hospital. A year and a day earlier, Dave received a phone call from his geology professor, Dr. Waterman (played by the science fiction/horror/fantasy writer Fritz Leiber), who gave no details but asked that

Dave come to his house and help him. Dave, all set to go on a picnic with his friend Jim (Frank Bonner, who later turned up as Herb on the sitcom *WKRP in Cincinnati*) and Jim's girlfriend, Vicki (Robin Christopher), decides to take them along to Dr. Waterman's place; Susan (Barbara Hewitt), a blind date for Dave, goes along too. After they find Waterman's home destroyed and Waterman himself missing, Dave and his pals explore the wooded area nearby, where they run into a creepy forest ranger (Woods, the director) who calls himself Asmodeus. Then they make their way into a cave, where a maniacally laughing old man hands them a large, leather-bound book containing mysterious symbols and writing in several languages. Also in it is a letter from Waterman, explaining that he found the ancient book in the Middle East and that its spells are meant to summon both good and evil spirits, in order to maintain a balance of light and dark in the world (like the equinox). Waterman, it seems, tried to summon spirits himself, unleashing the wrong ones—the monsters Dave and his friends soon meet; Asmodeus reappears, too, desperately wanting the book. Who is the old man in the cave, and why did he give the book to Dave and the others? Why does Asmodeus need a book for summoning evil spirits when he himself is the Devil? Why did Waterman call Dave in the first place? Hard to say.

Hard to say, too, what makes *Equinox* so watchable. Maybe it is the simple desire it arouses to see how all of its inept craziness will play out. Or maybe, as with the novels I read in high school, as with a Coltrane solo, what rivets is the sense of something behind what is seen or heard: these young filmmakers' operating out of sheer love of creating, calling loudly on the creative spirit, even if—like Dr. Waterman, like me—they sometimes found the spirit unresponsive, or summoned the wrong one. And maybe it's never too late to call on the right spirit. That is a conclusion you may reach if you live long enough, revisiting—like Coltrane does in "Equinox"—the same old themes, searching for something new.

Summer of '83

ON FAMILY, TRAVEL, WAR,

THE WOMEN OF YOUTH,

AND REDEMPTION

1.

The man I'll call Reverend Starks, friendly and forthright, tall and strong, was somewhere in his fifties when I worked for him in my hometown of Washington, D.C., that long-ago summer. I was back from Ohio between sophomore and junior years of college. The Baptist church Reverend Starks had founded years earlier, and still served as pastor, held summer-morning classes in its basement for a small handful of elementary school kids, all of them Black, like Reverend Starks and everyone associated with his church. I taught reading and math. In the afternoons I worked, often alone, in the church office upstairs, where there sometimes wasn't much to do beyond listening to pop songs made tinny by the little radio on my desk.

Reverend Starks, who was active in the church's lower-middle-class-to-poor community, would come and go. A couple of times he told me about my office work, "You're learnin'"—his kind way of saying that I could have done this thing or the other thing a little better but that, hey, I was young. Given how forceful he could be, in and out of the pulpit, I appreciated his forbearance, which stemmed in part from a sense of humor. Once, knowing that I was handy at lettering, he had me make a sign to put in the church window. Seeing that he was pleased with it, I offered to do others. "Don't want the place lookin' like a supermarket," he said with a smile.

On one rare occasion when he, too, was having a slow afternoon, Reverend Starks drifted out of his office and began talking—matter-of-factly and, it seemed to me, out of the blue—about his experiences in the South Pacific during World War II. He had lied about his age to enlist, which meant he was too young to have been seeing and doing the things he told me about. Then again, I have never met anyone old enough to see and do the things he told me about on that lazy summer afternoon.

2.

At twenty I was a little on the old side for what I had done at college that spring, which was to lose my virginity. The person I had lost it to, who was nineteen and white and whom I will call Joanne, had been my on-and-off girlfriend for a year and a half, the off parts owing entirely to me. In her abnormally shy, soft-spoken—make that whispery—way, Joanne was fiercely in love with me, but while I cared about her, or thought I did, or told myself I did, I wanted to date other people. Less than a year later, on my twenty-first birth-day, our relationship would end for good when she read my diary. In the meantime, though, her passion for me and my own lack of resolve were like fuel for a car that was not roadworthy, that followed a fitful pattern of going a ways, breaking down, and starting up again.

The comparison to the car is an odd one for me to make, since I did not then, and do not now, own one. When Joanne visited me at my mother's house that July, arriving by bus at night in a sketchy part of town inaccessible by Metro, I had to ask one of my high school friends to drive me to pick her up. What I remember most is what happened when the three of us were a couple of blocks from home. Joanne's skin color never meant much to me, and by that point in our relationship it meant nothing, but in this neighborhood it shone like the harvest moon. I was reminded of that when we passed a guy walking down the street. This was Derrick West, the twin brother of my old friend Dana, whom I hadn't seen in years. Recognizing me, seeing Joanne, Derrick stared at us in naked astonishment, and, as I saw when I turned around in my seat, he kept staring at us, his eyes following the car until we turned left onto my block.

3.

My mother's small house, where I had spent my entire childhood, was home to members of four generations: my long-widowed maternal grandmother, my widowed mother, one of my sisters, and my sister's daughter, who was under the age of two. That summer my sister, her daughter, and my grandmother shared a bedroom; I slept in the tiny room next to it; and down the short hall was my mother's room, where she slept during the day before her 10:30 p.m.-to-7:00 a.m. work shift.

My grandmother was the center of things. That makes her sound like the strong, domineering matriarch, who had the final say on everything. The opposite was true. Grandma, who was eighty-nine that summer, had been hard of hearing for as long as I could remember and by then was all but deaf, and because she couldn't hear herself, she tended to talk sparingly; she could not in good conscience be left alone for any length of time—and my family had nothing if not a conscience—and so it was not strength but disability that made everything revolve around her, that lent her small frame the gravitational pull of a heavenly body. You might think, too, that my sister was a single mother unable to afford her own place; in fact, she was not only married (though her husband lived elsewhere, which is her story to tell)—she was an associate at the prestigious law firm where she would later become a partner, before she left to become a judge. But someone had to stay with my grand-mother while my mother was at work and I was at college, so my sister stepped in. Two years later, when I graduated, I would return to D.C. and spend a year of my early twenties coming straight home from work to be with my grandmother; my sister moved back in when I left for New York.

If Grandma's helplessness arranged us all in an orbit around her, then her sweetness banished resentment as a sun banishes cold. She was too damn *cute* to resent—her white hair pulled back in a bun, her skinny tan legs coming down from her shapeless house dress like clappers from a bell, her breasts down around her waist, her humongous ears, her toothless mouth, her gravelly voice.

I have a memory of my grandmother sitting in a chair in our living room when Joanne came downstairs the first morning of her stay. The corners of Grandma's eyes crinkled as she gave a closed-mouth smile; while her upper arms stayed pinned to her sides, her thin forearms spread wide open, and Joanne, long straight brown hair, broad toothy smile, hugged her and knelt in front of her. The exchange between these two women, one young, one old, one Black, one white, one hearing, one deaf, went something like this:

"How are you?"

"Hi!" my grandmother said.

"It's good to see you!"

"Fine!"

Joanne, laughing, smitten, said when we were alone, "We got it all in there."

And much later, my grandmother—who never knew what any-body around her was talking about—said to me in private, "Poor Joanne. She loves you so."

4.

I have two sisters. The one who did not live at my mother's house that summer nonetheless came over often, visiting and helping out. This sister was, is, a mental-health professional. It was because of her that I knew Reverend Starks. She had begun attending his church in the company of her boyfriend; after the boyfriend drifted from her life, the church remained. (She would become its pastor after Reverend Starks's death, but that was far in the future.)

It was this sister who, late one night that summer, after my mother had left for work, drove the rest of us to the hospital when my grandmother fell ill. I have a vague memory of what was wrong with her—chills, fever, vomiting, all three? I do remember that her illness passed quickly, but not before the four of us, she and my sisters and me, spent the whole night in the emergency room, among people twitching in their restless half-sleep from drug overdoses or withdrawals.

Without having slept a minute, I went straight from there to teaching the kids at the church. I was in charge of three—all eight years old, two boys and a girl—who were just about the sweetest kids I'd ever met. They deserved a better teacher than they had that morning. One of the boys did, or failed to do, something—I have no memory of what—that could not possibly have called for all the yelling I did in response. My lasting memory is of his round, silent tears, clear marbles, falling onto his writing paper.

5.

The following winter Joanne would cry silent tears as I told her quietly, yet again, that I wanted to be free to see other people. Later that day, after tricking me into leaving her alone in my dorm room, she read my diary, freeing us both.

6.

A group of American soldiers in the South Pacific came upon a lone Japanese soldier. The group included Reverend Starks, who was not then a minister. What I don't remember from the story is whether the group knocked out the Japanese soldier's teeth before or after they cut off his head. In any case, the head was toothless when they posed for pictures with it, their own teeth showing in wide grins.

Perhaps to fill the silence caused by my loss for words, Reverend Starks said, "Nothin' worse than war."

7.

What is it with young men? What's that force in them that cannot be reasoned with, that must do, must go, with no thought for the right or wrong or even the where or the why of it?

The fuel of my relationship with Joanne, as I have written, was her love for me and my lack of resolve, but, oh, there was something else. And there was so much of it, once we started. Our hunger for each other's bodies led us to sneak to my mother's basement, and I recall Joanne's fright when she thought she heard the door opening and thought my kind mother would call her a slut. But it felt worth the risk.

In the fall, I would leave for a semester in London. You might think I read a lot about London before going, but I barely read a thing. Why was I not more interested in learning about this storied place where I would spend four months? How was it that I, a self-described writer about to travel to Great Britain, had come close that spring to failing a course called Survey of English Literature, 1700–1945? What made me want to travel to a place I seemed to have so little interest in learning about? Was it that simple blind force at work, the need to *go*, to *do*, to save the thinking for later, for someone else?

Often when we're young we have the perhaps unconscious belief that our real lives are still to come. The belief may be more of a wish: if life hasn't yet begun, how can it end? Perhaps the beginning of our goodness, sense, and wisdom—to the extent that we are good, sensible, and wise—is the realization that our lives are happening, that they have been all along, and that the lives of others are too.

I had glimmers of understanding this, walking aimlessly through the drizzle of London, past houses and pubs and Tube stops, worrying about my very old grandmother, from whom, for some reason, I had put myself an ocean away.

8.

Grandma died in 2000, when she was 106 and I was a thirty-seven-year-old father of two. Reverend Starks preached her funeral; he did the same when my mother died seven years later. The eulogies, particularly my grandmother's, were fire-and-brimstone sermons, Reverend Starks fairly roaring from the pulpit. On the night of the day my mother was buried, my nine-year-old younger daughter—to whom I had passed on no religious beliefs, having none myself by that point—said as she lay down to sleep, "He made me feel like I *have* to believe in God."

"Well," I said, sitting at the edge of her bed, "it's important to remember that being loud doesn't make you right."

The eulogies run together in my mind, except for one thing Reverend Starks said near the end of my grandmother's, his voice much calmer as he began a sentence with, "If you want to see her again . . ." I might have, arguably should have, been angry about that. I wasn't, somehow. I knew that he believed, passionately, what he was saying, and he was trying to do what he believed was needed above all else. To walk a path from the depths of wartime cruelty to the work of saving souls is to make quite a journey indeed. His own is a testament to the possibility of an awakening, a realization of the preciousness of human life, of the fragility of the loving human heart.

9.

At the end of the summer of 1983, when I left for London, my sisters took me to the airport. My mother and grandmother came out of the house and down the short walkway to see us to the car. And then I watched their backs as they returned to the house where I was raised, where they had instilled in me whatever seeds there were of goodness, sense, and wisdom. My eyes kept following them until they were gone.

On Rivers

ON FAMILY, JAZZ, POETRY,

THE PATH NOT FOLLOWED,

AND LOOKING BACK

One evening in the fall of 1982, when I was nineteen and in my sophomore year of college, a group of my fellow students and I, who should have been studying, sat in someone's dorm room and played a game. The game called for each person to pick three things—a favorite animal, a particular body of water, and one more thing, which I cannot remember—and describe them. Only when we were done did the game's initiator tell us what it all supposedly meant. In describing a bat, which I'd told the group was "cool, black, and awkward," I had summed up my view of myself. Just as eerily on the mark was what I'd said about the body of water, a description that represented my feelings about sex—which I was to have for the first time, technically speaking, about four months later, and about which I had developed a sense of wonder and apprehension that holy men bring to their contemplation of God and other eternal mysteries. The word I'd chosen was "murky."

The body of water I had thought of was a stream down the street from the house where I'd grown up. The word "stream" may bring to mind leisurely strolls along sun-dappled dirt roads with walls of trees to the left and right, but the area around this stream was a little different. I would glimpse the stream briefly, to my left and below me, as I walked across a little concrete overpass on my way to the bottom of Division Avenue to buy my *Spider-Man* and *Hulk* comic books at the drugstore. The store was part of a small commercial area near the intersection of Division and Nannie Helen Burroughs; there was a liquor store, a Safeway food market, the remains of a corner convenience store that had burned like kindling during the '68 riots, and not a lot more, aside from the small clusters of seemingly unemployed men hanging out here and there on the sidewalk. None of it was of much interest to a ten-year-old boy, so with my comic books in hand I would soon be on my way back up the hill. Maybe I would throw a glance toward the stream, but I never stopped to wonder, as I headed home to lose myself in superhero stories, where this thin, muddy, unimpressive trickle of water came from, or where it was going.

Rivers have been on my mind lately, though. Maybe it's more accurate to say that other things remind me of them. I am no longer nineteen, and the course of a life—as I am scarcely the first writer to observe—now seems to me river-like, in a number of ways; rivers, for example, pick up sediments in one place and deposit them in another, just as I have carried the memory of that little stream for four decades and given it to you to read about.

One of the many writers to take up the river theme is Langston Hughes, in his 1920 poem "The Negro Speaks of Rivers," written when he was seventeen:

> I've known rivers:
> I've known rivers ancient as the world and older than the
> flow of human blood in human veins.
>
> My soul has grown deep like the rivers.
>
> I bathed in the Euphrates when dawns were young.
> I built my hut near the Congo and it lulled me to sleep.
> I looked upon the Nile and raised the pyramids above it.
> I heard the singing of the Mississippi when Abe Lincoln

went down to New Orleans, and I've seen its muddy
bosom turn all golden in the sunset.

I've known rivers:
Ancient, dusky rivers.

My soul has grown deep like the rivers.

This poem is like a line from Shakespeare or a Bible verse, in that it is simple on one level and endlessly debatable on others. Is the speaker a single migratory soul, or the collective voice of humanity, past and present? The speaker may represent "Negro" humanity, as is certainly suggested by the title and the references to the Congo, the Nile, the Mississippi in the time of Abe Lincoln, and "dusky rivers," though the mention of the Euphrates casts some doubt on that notion. Or perhaps the speaker refers to the Euphrates ("when dawns were young") to evoke that mainstay of so many American Blacks and other Blacks, the Bible, in which the Euphrates is one of four rivers fed by the river flowing out of Eden—the others being the Tigris, the Pishon (thought by some to be the Ganges), and the Gihon (thought by some to be the Nile).

The Euphrates has in common with the Mississippi the fertile soil and corridors for transport that they provide to their respective regions. Such conditions—which ensure ready supplies of food and allow people to focus on matters beyond mere survival—make it possible for cultures to thrive among the people in those areas as they might not elsewhere. In the case of the Mississippi, that culture involves music, not least jazz.

The music that the Mississippi helped to produce is itself much like a river. The winding nature of a jazz sax solo, its flow over the piano/bass/drums accompaniment, makes me think of water curving through and around land, over rocks. Rivers have a horizontal dimension but also a vertical one, with water coming from above in the form of precipitation and from below, via groundwater sources; similarly, a horn solo is often a forward-moving melody with harmonic investigations that ascend and descend the chords. Braided rivers are so named because their waters split off and then rejoin each other; a musician playing a jazz version of a pop song creates much the same effect, departing from the existing melody to fashion another—and then, in the end, coming back to the main path.

On a Friday in the fall of 2013, I took a late bus from New York, my home of a quarter-century-plus, to D.C. I slept at my sister Phyllis's house, and the next morning she and I and my sister Wanda had a big breakfast at an IHOP. From there Phyllis and I drove to the bottom of Division Avenue, which was even more run-down than it had been during my boyhood, with one or two more abandoned buildings. In the midst of that blight, in the late-morning drizzle, we made an attempt to follow the course of the old stream I used to pass by so obliviously. I had unconsciously thought of the stream as beginning (or ending?) at the spot where I glimpsed it from the little paved overpass, but we traced its flow backward from there: we crossed Division, passed through a parking lot where the counterparts of those same men from decades ago stood around in clusters, and picked up the stream again, walking parallel to its bank, which was separated from us by thick weeds and bushes. Through gaps in that tangle of growth, we could see the brown water, maybe fifteen feet across, flowing in the opposite direction of our walk. Like much else in that area, in a touching attempt at revitalization, the footpath we were on—as a sign informed us—had been renamed for the late Marvin Gaye, a hometown boy. The path winds through residential streets with small houses; here and there we passed a lone man or woman, nearly all of them responding very warmly and helpfully when we asked how far the stream extended in both directions. One man we spoke with was raking leaves outside a small building called the Marvin Gaye Recreation Center. He told Phyllis and me that the water we were following had originally been called Watts Creek—Watts being the name of a land and slave owner. (Phyllis's Google search that evening confirmed that it is called Watts Branch stream.) The man said that he and others now called it Marvin Gaye Creek. We followed the water, whatever its name, a ways more, losing it here and picking it up there, once seeing an exposed length of it that was prettier than I would have thought, before coming to what we decided was as close to the beginning as we were going to get: the point where the stream was fed by water trickling out of two tunnels set a few feet apart beneath a small, muddy overhang. From there we walked back the way we had come and found Phyllis's car, then followed the stream in the direction it flowed, alternately driving and walking.

Phyllis, the sibling closest in age to me, is ten and a half years my senior. When we were, say, seven and seventeen, she seemed to me like a grownup, and so I have tended not to think of us as having grown up together. From the vantage point of fifty, though, seven and seventeen do not look very different in some ways, and as I was reminded during our journey along the stream, we have many memories in common. We talked about our parents and our grandmother, all of them gone now. We reminisced about the summer day camp where I was a student at the same time Phyllis was a teenaged counselor. We recalled the time that Grandma, a month shy of her eighty-fourth birthday, fell the length of the stairway on her way up to bed, destroying the wooden cabinet at the bottom of the stairs and cracking three ribs; and Phyllis reminded me of how the two of us ate dinner with Grandma in her room for many evenings after that, until she healed enough to go downstairs. At some point we touched on my high school and college days, and Phyllis had a belly laugh over the "cool, black, and awkward" bat and the "murky" water. We talked about her work—Phyllis is a judge—and compared notes on our children (collectively we have four daughters). And amid all that talk we traced the stream, again losing it for stretches, again glimpsing it through the growth along its banks before it disappeared underground once more, leading us to conclude, after more than two hours, that we had come to the end of what we could see.

Why had I wanted to follow the stream? In part it was simple, belated—very belated—curiosity about where it would lead. No doubt, though, there were other things at work, too, not least likely the final tremors of a midlife crisis. There is no percentage in regretting the past, and one life, even a full one, can contain only so much, but these well-worn truths are easier to know than to believe.

The path along the stream was a literal example of Frost's road not taken, and in following it, I think I was giving a nod to its more figurative brothers: those other murky avenues that I was too thoughtless, or too self-absorbed, or too timid, or too busy with something else to explore. It is the "too busy with something else" that I hold onto in the end, because you can lead only one life, and it can take all your energy to figure out what that one is about and try to proceed accordingly.

All your energy, plus a little luck. After Phyllis and I ended our journey along the stream, she drove me to the bus station. We were on the Benning Road overpass when we saw, stretching out below and to our left, wide and brown, the Anacostia River—which flows into the Potomac. Those greater bodies of water, it turned out, are where our stream leads, making its little contribution, or so we think, at a point just beyond our seeing.

New York

Long Red Monte Carlo

ON LEAVING HOME
AND FINDING ONE'S WAY

I have owned one car in my life. I bought it used from my older brother in late 1985, when I was twenty-two. The car was a long red Monte Carlo with white trim. In the years before that, after our father died, my brother—fourteen years my senior and a man when I was a boy—would show up in that car and drive me, and sometimes my friends, or his friends, or my sister, to sports events in D.C. or to Baltimore Orioles baseball games. In the car we would talk and joke and laugh, once in a while even sing. I had good times in that car.

Now it was mine. I had bought it because . . . I was not really sure why I bought it. At the time I had a job in Georgetown, which I could get to with perfect ease on the Metro. Generally speaking, there were not many places I went that required a car. I suppose I thought that I was now an adult—never mind that, after I graduated from college in Ohio, my bachelor's degree and I went straight back to live in my mother's house—and that being an adult meant having a car. Needing or wanting to drive it was secondary.

And deep down, I didn't want to drive it. A lot of people love the feel and freedom of driving—certainly our culture celebrates those things—but those were outweighed for me by other factors, chief

73

among them the astounding ease with which I can get lost. I thought about writing that I have the country's or the world's worst sense of direction, but that would suggest the presence of said sense. If getting lost were an ability, I would be Captain America, and behind the wheel I am Superman himself, my already phenomenal capabilities increased exponentially, allowing me to travel at the speed of thought from familiar environments to those where my lack of orientation is total, where up may as well be down, left is the same as right. Things are worse at night. Once—once—I drove to work; that was harrowing enough, but then, after the sun had gone down, I set out for home. A wrong turn somewhere, a few minutes of moving in a bad direction much more quickly than humans were built to move, and I could have been in outer space for all that I recognized. I had a moment of absolute and absolutely frightening clarity, the realization that, even as I did not know and could barely see where I was going, my every decision and indecision was determining the path of two speeding tons of metal. I saw one older man, caught in my headlights in that darkness, standing on a divider and starting to cross; then he spotted me and danced back the other direction, his face that of one who has seen death. Somehow, I do not know how, I made it home and did not kill anyone that I know of on the way, and I returned the next day to public transportation, which I began calling "Metro, my buddy."

I wonder, now, what would have happened if I had remained in D.C. Would I eventually have shed my fears, developed a sense of where I was going, and become comfortable behind the wheel like everyone else? Or would I simply have sold the car and kept riding the Metro? As it happened, a confluence of events set me on a third path. That spring of 1986, when I had turned twenty-three, the bottom fell out of both my plans to obtain an MFA in fiction writing and my long-distance romance with my college girlfriend. In danger of disappearing down a hole of doubt as to whether I could do anything at all, I sold the Monte Carlo and moved—though not for this reason—to perhaps the one place in these United States where no one needs a car.

And so began my three-decades-and-counting relationship with the

New York City subway. The rush-hour commute from Brooklyn to Manhattan on the F train, which soon became routine, was a marvel to me in those early days; if the aim had been not to reach our respective destinations but to find out how many people could be jammed together butt-to-butt in a train car, everybody breathing in what somebody else had just breathed out, the result would have looked exactly the same, each of us straining to hold on to a pole—for mysterious reasons, since the one thing less likely than finding a comfortable position in that human sardine tin was falling down. The magic of the New York subway is that you no sooner get used to one element than it throws another at you, and I use the word "magic" advisedly, because, like a magician, the subway can seemingly produce anything. It is not news that on any given trip you are likely to see a singer, or a saxophonist, or a preacher, or a comedian, or a team of acrobats—some of them pretty good—or some combination of these. Then there are the more unusual sights. The first I remember was on a downtown platform at West Fourth Street, where my eye fell on a man I slowly realized was wearing exactly one article of clothing: the green leather jacket that covered only the upper reaches of the crack in his rear end. And there was what I saw one June day in 1988 on the D train, which continues to amaze me not because it happened but because, despite the great variety and sheer number of people who pour into the subway each day, I haven't seen it happen more often. A man was sleeping, his body spread across five seats on a fairly crowded car. The train stopped at a station in Midtown Manhattan, and a man who got on saw the sleeper and slapped his foot. The sleeper sat up and said, groggily and angrily, "What you wake me up for?" The two men got into a shouting match, which quickly turned into a fistfight. The sleeper, who had begun to lose the fight, left the train, which was being held in the station, and the other man took a seat. A few moments later the sleeper returned, holding a glass bottle. "You wanna fight now?" he said to the other man, bringing the bottle with great force down on the man's head, creating an explosion of glass and blood—especially blood.

More important for me than the subway's ability to surprise, though, is another trait, the opposite of that one: its constancy.

Friendships and other relationships in New York began and ended; I worked here, and then I worked there, and then I worked somewhere else; I had an apartment in this neighborhood, then that neighborhood, then another, and then the first again, and through it all, there was, there has been, the subway. I rode it every day in the course of discovering that there were, in fact, things I could do, among them thriving at a job, finding a life partner, raising children. And while thriving at a job can be a trap—do one thing well and you may find yourself supervising those who do it less well, your stress mounting until you sing along with David Byrne, "Well, how did I get here?"—the subway was there for that too. These days the subway announcements are automated, but for a time, on the uptown number 4 train, there was a live person telling you where you were and saying to those getting off, somehow accenting the last two words equally, in the same, near-musical tone, "Have a great, daaaayy. . ." I have no idea what this conductor looked like, and to be honest I don't even know if I was hearing a man or a woman. But I do remember that on those mornings when I was on my way to run my department, maybe facing a tight deadline, or an uncomfortable talk with a staff member, or a meeting that was sure to be aggravating, or all three, I would hear "Have a great, daaaayy . . . .," and I would be cheered just a little and think, "Okay—*sniff*—I'll try!"

But even constancy is not the subway's greatest gift to me. In 1993, having moved into the Brooklyn home where I still live, I began working in the Bronx, making for a solid forty-five minutes of train time, twice a day. I was struggling for some semblance of success as a writer, another journey on which I felt lost; part of that journey was reading as much as I could, and on those trains to and from the Bronx, as slow a reader as I am, I put away hundreds upon hundreds of books by great writers, from John Cheever to Tolstoy to Ishmael Reed, from Jane Austen to Colson Whitehead to Zadie Smith, feeling each work add muscle to the lean frame of my literary understanding. (At home I read essays and other nonfiction and sometimes poems, but being on a moving train seemed to call for the forward motion of fiction.) One Saturday in the mid-2000s I biked with my older daughter around Prospect Park to her soccer game; as I stood on the sidelines watching, my mind drifted toward my reading life. I was forty-one years old at the time, and the soccer coach, I happened to know, was sixty-one—and watching him run around on the field, twenty years older than I was and still very vital, I thought of how many good years I had ahead of me, and how much time I could spend reading and learning (particularly if I continued to work in the Bronx, which I did for seven more years), and I felt a quiet surge of joy.

And yet. One day many years ago a coworker said in my presence that you don't feel like an adult until you have a business card. (At the time I was in my twenties and several years away from having my first business card, and the comment annoyed me greatly.) And I realize now, in a way I somehow couldn't articulate when I was twenty-two, that a car is a kind of two-ton business card. A card announces to the world that some entity, somewhere, has found you worthy of representing it in a position of ostensible importance, a signifier of your capability; a car announces to the world that you have an adult's ability to determine your own course, to follow your own plan and carry it out.

My experience with cars did not end with the Monte Carlo, and yet the nature of that experience does not confirm what is supposedly confirmed by sole ownership of a car. In my case a car does not represent independence because, as I like to say, my wife (who has a sense of direction) and I (who somehow has a license) together make up one driver. We've had some good times that way, though. I remember in particular the feeling of driving a rental car in the mountains out West, under that big sky, the sense of possibility as my wife sat in the passenger seat beside me, pregnant with our first child. (About seven years later that same child, our older daughter, looking out of our apartment window at the rental car I had driven home in preparation for a beach vacation, asked me—with no trace of facetiousness but with genuine curiosity and, perhaps, the slightest hint of concern—"Do you know how to drive?" As a young adult she took driving lessons. "Try to remember what your parents do in the car," the instructor told her.

"You don't understand," she replied.)

It is important to realize, of course, that symbols such as cars and business cards are merely that—symbols—and should not be confused with the things they represent. And yet symbols have a certain importance of their own, and so it is also important to understand that there are different ones. Several years ago I began teaching creative nonfiction writing at a college north of New York City. To get there I take the subway to a commuter train. On that train, with a seat to myself, looking out the window at suburbs whizzing by, my briefcase next to me and my fedora in the overhead rack, I feel a bit like a Cheever character; that is to say, I feel—in a way I somehow never have before—like an adult.

I close with two memories. The first is a memory of the climax of one of my favorite movies, *The Graduate*. A friend of mine once said that every man in America wants to be Dustin Hoffman's character, Ben, as he roars down highways and back roads in his sports car to stop his beloved Elaine from getting married. But then he runs out of gas and has to finish the trip on foot.

The second is a memory from the spring of 1986, when I was twenty-three. I had already seen my college romance and my grad school plans go south, but I had not yet moved to New York; marriage, children, and a career were all years away. I still owned the long red Monte Carlo, and one Sunday I drove two good friends and the girlfriend of one of them to a Baltimore Orioles game. We had just taken our seats at the stadium when two people, one of them a woman in her early thirties, sat next to us, the woman's seat adjacent to mine. She struck up a conversation with me. As I discovered later, she also caught the first name of one of my friends as well as a reference to where he worked. The next day, at home, I answered the phone. The caller said, "This is the woman who sat next to you at the baseball game." A few nights after that, I set out in the Monte Carlo for her apartment in a Virginia suburb. I made my way there uncertainly, operating less on knowledge than on dim faith—based on what, I could scarcely tell you now.

The Home of Two Cliffs

ON FINDING ONE'S WAY

AND FATHERING

My older daughter and I were biking around Brooklyn's Prospect Park to her last soccer game of the season, she in her pale green uniform. The spring of 2003, this was. I had turned forty a couple of months before. My daughter was nine. If memory serves, it was during this ride that she asked if I played sports as a kid, if my father was involved, what all of that was like.

"My father thought it was important for me to know how to play baseball," I said as we pedaled in the pleasant air around the park's paved inner loop. "People in his generation thought there were some things boys should just know how to do. So he tried to teach me. We spent a lot of time playing catch in our backyard. I wasn't very good at it at first. And he wasn't well—he was a good dozen years older than I am now, and he was in pain a fair amount of the time. He died within a couple of years of that. But he thought it was important for him to do this while he still could, because he knew he didn't have a lot of time. When I messed up, he got impatient, and sometimes a little nasty. He was in pain, like I said. I understand it all now, but at the time I hated it, and I resented it. So, that was my experience with sports as a kid."

We came to what I called, in my head, Dead Man's Hill—the steep decline we had to bike down before exiting the park at the Parade Grounds. This part of the ride always made me nervous. I worried that my daughter would panic at how quickly she was moving and lose control of her bike somehow; I pictured a horribly scraped or broken arm, a head injury despite her helmet. But I didn't tell her to be careful, as I was tempted to do, because I didn't want her to be afraid. We coasted down the hill in silence, slowing as we always did when the road mercifully flattened out. Soon we reached the field where her team would be playing.

On the soccer field, parents and uniformed girls stood around, mostly quiet, waiting for the doughy, brown-haired coach. "Good morning," I said, for some reason, as he and his daughter, who was on the team, walked onto the field. Old habits die hard, I guess. "How are *you*," he said, as joylessly as usual, no question mark, because it was the very last thing he wanted to know. The team photo, which we would all receive later, told me I should not take it personally: his face, as he stood by the girls, was the face of someone who has spent hours outside the operating room and is finally about to talk to the surgeon.

The coach, as always, asked for a parent volunteer to be a linesperson. I took a couple of steps back. I had done this before, and I hated it. When the ball went out of bounds, as it frequently did, the linesperson called which team had last had contact with it, determining which team should have it now. You could say the stakes were not high. Still, this was a job that called for someone with complete confidence in his judgment or, failing that, the belief that being decisive was more important than being right.

I was the opposite of that person. I once heard *liberal* defined as someone who won't take his own side in an argument, and to some extent that was me, a person who would do anything before he would risk being in the wrong. This seeming self-effacement may in fact be a kind of egotism, the conviction that one knows what the rights and wrongs of a situation *are*, that one is above the rest of squabbling humanity.

Convictions are tricky. To be without them is to live, at best, a meaningless life. To follow a conviction too devotedly—say, the conviction that your son should learn to play baseball come hell or high water—can do more harm than good.

How had I managed this balance in my life, up to age forty? The answer could lie, or not, in a quick glance at that life. I had a decent job and was happily married and raising two girls I adored in a beautiful neighborhood. At the same time, there were things I dreamed of and pursued but felt very far from achieving. Did I have the balance right, or had I gone wrong somewhere, followed the wrong conviction or not followed the right one? There were times when I thought of my life as a giant machine, one that I had built but that was now controlling my actions with merciless regularity, regardless of what I might want or any convictions I might have. There were other times, in the few hours I had to myself, when I wrote or read or watched a film or listened to music, when I felt as one with the creative spirit.

What would my father have done?

This is the person I was, this was the life I lived, these were the questions I asked as I stood on the sidelines and cheered for my daughter's soccer team. After the game was over, the parents and kids all met at the coach's house to have pizza and celebrate the season. The coach and his daughter lived not far from my apartment—one street over and a few blocks down the hill that gives Park Slope its name. The house, a brownstone, was near the bottom of its block. The house number seemed familiar. When we walked in, I looked around at the layout and the high tin ceilings. In the same moment I realized, and said aloud to whoever was near, "I used to live here." And for a moment, like a character in a science fiction series, I was transported to another time, another life, another self.

The time was seventeen years earlier, the late summer and early fall of 1986, when I was twenty-three and new to the city and living on the top floor of this very brownstone. I shared it with another man, a thirty-year-old who, like me, was named Cliff. This all might have come from the mind of a sitcom writer, since our first names were the beginning and end of what we had in common. Actually, that's not true—we were both thin, and neither of us was exactly tall. Otherwise, imagine *The Odd Couple* with both guys named Oscar. I was introverted, quiet, and, incidentally, Black, with close-cropped hair; my roommate was extroverted, loud, and, incidentally, white (and Jewish), with stringy blond hair that came to his shoulders. Cliff rented the top floor from the family downstairs, and I rented the larger of the two bedrooms from Cliff (his room was tiny); we shared a kitchen, bathroom, and living room. When I moved in, my roommate cheerfully changed the message on the answering machine to say, "This is the home of TWO Cliffs!" We shared other things too. I had a turntable and a stack of albums—rock, R&B, a few classical—that I put in the living room. One day Cliff told me he had rearranged my albums. "It's a simple system," he said with a grin. "See if you can figure it out." When I couldn't, he told me: he put the ones he liked on top. He felt I should be free with his things too. Once I asked if I could borrow or use something, I forget what. "You don't gotta ask," he told me. "Just do." Cliff's laugh sounded a lot like a car engine revving. When a friend of mine from back home visited, he and I and Cliff and Cliff's girlfriend went to see *She's Gotta Have It* at the old theater on Flatbush Avenue; the movie made Cliff laugh, and my friend was more entertained by my roommate than by Spike Lee. "Coolest white boy I ever met," he later told me.

When I knew him, Cliff didn't have a job—"I'm livin' on spit," he said at one point—and/but he was an aspiring pop musician. "If it's not Top 40, I'm not interested," I heard him tell a potential collaborator. He sang—yowled, really—and played guitar, and he would play me the songs he wrote. That was how I discovered that you can get songs stuck in your head, and find yourself singing them, whether you like them or not.

What about the other Cliff, the one speaking to you now? I would write short stories, typing them up on the manual typewriter I had bought for seven bucks at the local flea market. (On a few occasions my roommate read and critiqued them, thoughtfully.) I worked for a company in Manhattan, where I was my department's low man on the totem pole—that may have been my title—a job in which, unlike future jobs that involved more responsibility, I never knew from one hour to the next what would be coming at me. I didn't like that much. I didn't like the pay, either. One of the measly twice-monthly paychecks covered the rent, or most of it, and the other covered everything else, or didn't—I can remember stuffing laundry into a pillowcase because a pillow seemed beyond my means.

The unpredictability of life in those days, at work and outside it, had the occasional upside. I recall going out for the evening with a casual female friend, an occasion I didn't think of as a date until, as we were having coffee, our hands accidentally touched on the table, and neither of us pulled away.

All of this is to say that I hadn't yet built the machine, the one that ran my life with such regularity. That had its problems. If I didn't know from day to day what was happening in my world externally, that was partly because I wasn't too sure what was going on inside, either. I had convictions—about the unimportance of race, the oneness of people—that I had not thought through very far. What would later be my interests in film and music were more impulses then, blind groping. To put it more succinctly, there was a lot I didn't know about who I was, and knowing who you are makes difficulties on every level easier to deal with.

I wonder, now, if that accounts for the inordinate fright I felt late one night in my room, when summer had become fall, when I was on the edge of sleep and suddenly heard a rustling I thought was a rat under the floor or in the wall. I went to get the other Cliff. As we stood in my room, he explained in a groggy but kindly voice—I had woken him up—that the heat was coming on, that there was nothing to worry about. In that one moment I felt comforted, cared for. Fathered.

A young woman I was close to at the time said once that Cliff had a big heart. I realized she was right. I liked him, though if I was being honest I would have said that I liked the *idea* of him, that there were days I wished he would practice his big-heartedness, and his loudness, and his voice exercises ("I-love-you-TRU-u-u-ly"), and his midnight sessions with his girlfriend, and his freedom with other people's things, away from where I lived. I was beginning to learn that much about myself. So I wasn't altogether dismayed when Cliff told me after three months that the landlord wanted to give the top floor to a family member, and the two of us needed to leave. "Welcome to New York," he said. I moved out, in the casual way of the young—that brownstone was the third of five places I lived in when I was twenty-three—and went elsewhere in the neighborhood, and then places out of the neighborhood, starting on the road that brought me, seventeen years later, to an afternoon pizza party with my daughter and her teammates and their parents and the coach.

As we sat and stood eating pizza, the coach talked about the people who volunteered as referees for the American Youth Soccer Organization. "It's one thing if your kid is on the team, and you're a coach for that reason," he said. "But being a referee—that's just pure altruism."

So, this man's being a coach was an extension of what he saw as his responsibility as a parent. Not being particularly charismatic, he was better at some parts of this job than others. But who fills all roles equally well?

And I thought of something I had witnessed earlier in the soccer season. The team's win/loss record was not impressive, but during a break near the end of one game, the coach gathered the girls and told them, "It's looking like we're going to win this game. So it's important for us to be gracious about it."

We learn gradually about ourselves, and our selves, and we do what we can. Sometimes it works better than other times, this rising of our different selves to meet different roles. My old roommate had called the top floor of the brownstone "the home of two Cliffs"; my body was, is, the home of more than two Cliffs, probably many more, and who knew how many other people. Somewhere in me was my father, a man I never really got to know, and he was only the beginning. Occasionally I think of the people I will never know about. Was there, centuries ago in Africa, an ancestor who watched his daughter climb higher and higher in a tree, who felt afraid for her but did not want to make her afraid by saying so? How much of the machine is genetic? From time to time I look in the mirror and wonder what other people are looking back at me.

But we can deal only with what we know. At forty I began to think of my father not as one who had made my life miserable for misguided reasons, but as one who thought he had a job to do and tried to do it the best he could. As I looked more kindly on him, I began to father myself. I'm not sure I ever told my daughter that part of the story. I will have to, one of these days.

Life with Rodents

ON FATHERING
AND LEAVING HOME

1.

I knew something was wrong as soon as I walked into my apartment. Straight ahead of me was the short hallway, from which nothing else in the place was visible, but the *flap . . . flap* from the other side of the wall at the far end told me what was happening. I turned on the hall light and steeled myself. When I laid out the rectangular, bright yellow glue traps with their white plastic borders, I knew I would have to deal with the results, but of course the guaranteed outcome of any situation is the one you can't foresee; I had been surprised days earlier when I found gray fur on one of the traps, from a now partially bald mouse who had a story to tell his many buddies, but here was something worse: not an uncaught rodent, but a half-caught rodent.

I was in something of a trap myself. It was 1987. In the summer of the previous year, I had moved to New York, having landed an entry-level job with a book publishing company. Through ads in the *Village Voice* in those pre-internet days, I had found roommates in trendy Park Slope (the other Cliff, for example), but after six months of that succession of lunatics, I felt—introvert that I was—ready to go it alone. The question was how to afford my own place on my miserable salary. My solution was to move into a one-bedroom apartment so far out in Brooklyn that most native New Yorkers I talked to had heard of neither the neighborhood (Cypress Hills, near the border of Queens) nor the subway train I took to get out there (the J). I had wanted to be alone; well, I got my wish. As a college-educated twenty-four-year-old Black man in this lower-middle-class Hispanic neighborhood, I both fit in and didn't, having friendly interactions with neighbors and my landlord—whose sister ran the Laundromat downstairs, where I dropped off my clothes—but getting to know no one. My place was so far from anything at all that I had very infrequent visits from friends, every one of whom asked at some point, having spent a shockingly long time in transit to see me, "How did you *find* this place?" A great divide existed between my work life, my social life, and my love life—such as that was—on the one hand, and where I lived, on the other; I felt I was commuting between universes.

And yet I wasn't quite alone out there. On my very first morning in the place, I rose in my very own bedroom and gave a satisfied glance at the living room—all mine!—on my way to the kitchen, where I saw a quick movement that I told myself, and almost managed to believe, was my imagination. But my imagination could not have produced what I saw in the days and weeks that followed. I was, almost literally, overrun. I saw them scamper, two and three at a time, across the kitchen floor (I started to write *my* kitchen floor, but that would be inaccurate); I saw them disappear down into my stove, tails waving like blades of grass in the wind as they crawled beneath the burners; I saw one flatten its body, in a way I would not have believed had I just heard about it, to fit between the kitchen counter and the wall; and I once woke in the night to the sound of rattling, which turned out to be one of them investigating the container of cookies I had left on my bedside table, maybe a foot from my face.

This was war.

And so here I was, both general and foot soldier in this war, back from Friday night socializing in the city, standing in the middle of my hallway, working up the nerve to finish what I'd started. I gave myself a final mental push and went to the end of the hall, turned left into the living room, then right to the kitchen. Sure enough. Left legs on the trap, right legs free, it alternately rose and crashed, as if having grown a too-heavy extension of itself. I went to my bedroom for a long piece of wood, left over from the three bucks' worth of lumber I had bought to build myself a rickety bookcase. A couple of raps on the head—each one producing a squeal—and it was done. I opened a brown paper grocery bag and froze my nerves long enough to pick up the trap by one edge and drop it, along with the little flopping gray body, inside. I rolled the top so I couldn't see the bag's contents. And I wonder now, from a distance of three-plus decades, what went through the head of that young man with my name as he stood there, so alone, with his freshly killed mouse. Did he long for someone to tell about it? Did he envision a time when he would not face such things alone? Did he look to a day when he would cohabitate not with mice or lunatics but with people he cared about, who cared about him? Did he have faith that he would find them?

2.

Nineteen years later. I was forty-three. It was the spring of 2006, and I was again living in an apartment in Park Slope—my home of fifteen years—which I shared with my wife and our two daughters.

On this particular evening my wife was out. I was in a room by myself, watching a DVD rental, Antonioni's *The Passenger*. In the next room, my older girl was cavorting with her fellow twelve-year-olds, guests for a sleepover. My younger daughter, seven, was probably cowering elsewhere in the apartment.

I was not to finish watching *The Passenger* that evening. At one point the girls' shouts and shrieks—which I had managed to tune out as background noise—took on a new tone, and I went to the living room to see what was happening. The four girls, looks of astonishment on their faces, were gathered around the cage containing my daughters' two hamsters. Both rodents, Apollo and Scurry, were female—or so we thought, until that evening. I looked in the cage. Apollo was on her back, surrounded by several pink blobs: her babies.

In the next few minutes, amid a lot of prepubescent loudness, two unfortunate things occurred. I got some bad advice; and I took it.

"We have to take the babies out!" one of the girls insisted. "The mother will eat them otherwise!" Well, I certainly didn't want us all to see that, and this girl seemed to know more about hamsters than I did. As is obvious in retrospect, mother hamsters cannot always—or even usually—eat their young, or else there would be no hamsters at all, but in the heat of the moment I did not think things through that far. Not one to touch rodents myself, I directed the girls to remove the apparently male Scurry from the scene (he was deposited in a carrying case) and to place the babies on top of some paper towels on a metal tray from the kitchen.

Now there was a new problem: having "saved" the five or so little pink babies from their mother, how would we keep them alive?

I called friends in the neighborhood, a fellow family of hamster owners, for guidance. That was how I came by the phone number of a woman whose real name I have forgotten—if I ever learned it—but whose nickname has stayed with me: the Rodent Lady. "Your big mistake was taking them out of the cage," the Rodent Lady told me. "You can't put them back in, because the mother will sense they've been tainted by humans and kill them. So you'll have to keep them alive on your own. You've got your work cut out for you." She was not wrong about that. On her instructions, I went to the grocery store to buy ready-made yellow baby (human) formula, which I was to dispense to the tiny newborn hamsters with an eye dropper every hour, all night, as they lay on their backs under the heat of a lamp, looking like pink tokens from a children's board game. I may have, sometime during the course of my life, slept worse than I did that night; then again, I may not have. Once an hour, more bleary-eyed each time, I went to the kitchen to give out the drops, and while I thought I saw their mouths moving to take in the formula, it may have been wishful thinking, or a dream. In the morning, I set out with the tray of baby hamsters to the veterinarian ten blocks from my home. I had walked about three-quarters of the way when I noticed something. The babies were all dead.

At about that time I came to a trash can, and I tossed them in.

Two or three months later—a summer evening.

My family and I returned by commuter train from Amagansett, New York, where we had spent the night with friends who had a summer house. We walked into the apartment, ready to settle back in our routine. Something was not quite right, though. Apollo (our older daughter's pet) and Scurry (our younger daughter's) now lived in separate cages; we had borrowed Scurry's cage from still more friends in the neighborhood, who had, as I recall, gotten it secondhand themselves. Its mileage had begun to show, and sometimes tape was needed to keep the cage closed. And sometimes, as we were about to discover the hard way, even tape didn't do the trick.

"I don't want to be an alarmist," I said, looking in the cage, "but I don't see Scurry."

A long search ensued. It was still in progress when our daughters' bedtime rolled around. They were asleep when my wife spotted Scurry in the act of, well, scurrying along the baseboard in the hallway and scooped him up. She woke our younger daughter, who saw Scurry and went back to sleep with a smile on her face.

That wasn't the end of the trouble, though. Over the next few days, Scurry started looking funny, most noticeably developing a red growth on his head. I realized with horror, and whispered to my wife, that Scurry could well have gotten into the mouse poison we had put around the apartment. My wife took him to the vet (the same vet I hadn't quite made it to with the baby hamsters); the vet gave Scurry a shot—"which he didn't like a bit," my wife reported—and said he should be fine.

Then came the night before our younger daughter's eighth birthday. She and her sister were in the living room watching TV; I passed by the room where Scurry's cage was and thought I'd look in on him. He wasn't moving. I grabbed a ruler and gently poked him.

The ruler met not with the pliancy of flesh but with the stiffness of a piece of driftwood. At about that time my wife passed the doorway, and I motioned to her to come in and told her the news. She took a moment, grabbed my arm, lowered her head, and shivered. Then we hatched our plan. It was simply out of the question to tell our daughter, hours before her birthday, that her pet was dead. So, after the girls went to bed, I would take Scurry, cage and all, to the basement to be put out with the garbage. The next day, we would explain to the girls that after they went to bed, Scurry had started behaving oddly, so we had taken him to the vet, where they would keep him for a day or so; our younger daughter could enjoy her birthday, confident that her pet would return soon. When her birthday was over, we would tell her what had happened—the relevant part, at least.

The plan went as well as it could have, given the way it had to conclude. As I headed to the basement with the cage, though, I wondered if I would ever have an encounter with a rodent that didn't involve killing it, accidentally or otherwise.

3.

I have had many adventures with my wife and daughters. Most of them have not involved rodents. Most of them, while of no particular interest to an outside party, are treasure to my aging heart. Like every family man, I have known exasperation. Mainly what I have known, though, is joy. And I have never, once, felt alone.

As children do, though, mine have grown up and left. My younger daughter, on going to college, left two gerbils behind, both definitely female: April, with her gray and white fur, and Charlie, whose coat was black. When we brought them home, back in the spring of 2014, April seemed the shyer one, hiding a lot in the big replica of a peanut shell in their tank, while Charlie seemed generally more comfortable. As time went on, though, the two appeared to switch personalities: April came out of her shell, so to speak, and was very relaxed when my daughter picked her up and let her run along her arms and shoulders, while Charlie was more skittish. Even April and Charlie's relationship to each other appeared to change; April became more assertive, giving at least as good as she got when it came to the way they sniffed and licked each other. What never changed, though, was how close they were. They made up each other's world.

Then, in the spring of 2017, April died. (Her death was the result of natural causes; she was three years old, a Methuselah in the world of gerbils.) With my daughter off at college, I put on rubber gloves and removed April from the tank. In her absence, Charlie did what I had never seen her do: she lay on her side, panting. Watching her, I was sure she would die soon, too. To my surprise, she recovered and lived for about half a year more. But as she lay there, her tiny body visibly giving way to grief at the departure of one so close, I thought I knew just a little of what she felt.

La Bohème

On a Saturday or Sunday afternoon in the early, cold months of 1988, I sat alone at a table for two in a Greenwich Village diner, twenty-four years old, hopelessly young, my notebook open in front of me. At the table next to mine were three people, all white: a woman and her very young daughter, and, across from them, another woman, who talked to the child in a kind way. I recall thinking that this woman was good with kids. When the mother took her little girl to the restroom, the other woman turned to me.

"What are you working on?" she asked.

I'm sure I smiled—that is what I did with everyone, that is what I do. "Trying to write a short story," I said.

"I thought so from the way you looked," she said. "I know that feeling of trying to get something on paper"—and she imitated my expression of paralyzed urgency. We laughed. We talked a little about writing. And at some point, apparently, I told her my first name and where I worked.

Where I worked: Quite a few young people take entry-level jobs at publishing houses because they love books and also, often, secretly or not-so-secretly, want to write them. They sometimes learn the hard way that their passions have very little to do with the day-to-day business of making and publishing books. This is a way of saying that I didn't love my job. But I needed to earn a living—meager though it was—and I was at my desk, ostensibly doing that, two or three days after my visit to the diner, when my phone rang.

"This is Liz," the caller said. She added, clearing up my confusion and handing me a surprise too, "We met in the restaurant the other day." We talked for a few minutes, by the end of which we had agreed that I would come to her apartment in the Village that Saturday night.

Where do I begin describing the young man who went to Liz's place? Let's start with how he looked: Darker than some Black folks, lighter than some others. A few people, on meeting him, thought he was a teenager, because of his face and also, probably, because he was on the small side—five feet eight inches and skinny, 150 pounds or so, though with a small pot belly he tried to suck in. There were other parts of his body he wasn't crazy about; he had the thinnest wrists and legs he knew of—he avoided wearing shorts and swimming trunks when possible—and the less said about his chin, the better. Partly for those reasons, partly for others, this young man's manner did not scream "confidence." At this point you may not be thinking "woman magnet," and yet our young man was not without experience in that area; he had had half a dozen or so lovers, including two with whom he had been in serious relationships. He was nothing if not nice, which can sometimes carry the day, though hardly always. If it seems mysterious that this guy had had any luck at all with women, the mystery may be cleared up, or possibly deepened, by what a woman at his previous job had once told him: "I've never met anybody as good-looking and as underconfident as you are." He might have dismissed the "good-looking" part, except that he'd heard it from other people: a diner waitress in the town where he'd gone to college, who told him, unprompted, "You are really handsome"; a group of young girls in the same town, who stared at him from across the park where he sat with his date, girls who giggled and shrieked before getting up their nerve to come over and say, "You look like Michael Jackson!" (We could go into what various women did to this young man on subway cars, but that may need its own essay. Plus, nobody would believe it.)

None of this helped his confidence, at least outwardly, and yet, in there somewhere, he had some. It was a kind of forward-looking confidence, not about what he could do in the moment but what he would do some day yet a ways off, and it, this confidence, was not only present but completely, absurdly out of proportion to any evidence. Writing would be involved. He wanted to write—he *did* write—and he believed strongly that it would lead him somewhere. He had a lot to learn, and he knew it, and in his groping way he went about trying to learn: reading novels, seeking out screenings of classic films that he often attended alone, going here and there to an art museum.

This was the young man who made his way on a Saturday evening to Liz's apartment. He—I—took the subway in from Cypress Hills. No doubt, as I sat among other Black and Brown folks on the lumbering J train, I had a novel or a story collection with me; no doubt, too, I was distracted from my already slow reading by thoughts of the evening to come. Who knows, this might be the start of a relationship. I hadn't been in a serious one since I'd come to New York, a year and a half earlier. Part of the reason had to do with my approach to pursuing women, which was really no approach at all. It would be easy to put that down to a lack of confidence, but the real explanation is more complicated. In high school I had a crush on a girl, Cheryl was her name, and I asked my mother (my father was four or five years dead by then) if I ought to tell Cheryl how I felt. No, she said; she recommended going slow, trying to figure out first how Cheryl felt about me, because if I opened my heart to her blindly, "She might tell her friends, and they might laugh at you." This was loving, well-intended, but unfortunate advice (for one thing, I realized later that Cheryl would have happily become my girlfriend if I had only said the word, and it seems everyone knew this but me), and it was advice for which I do not blame my mother one bit. Good parents—and my mother was a good parent— communicate to their children what they have come to understand, but no one understands everything, and it is on the kid, eventually, to learn some things for his, her, their self. But I will say that my mother's advice fortified my unconscious, unfortunate feeling that there was something embarrassing, something shameful, about admitting that you wanted to be with another person, unless that person clearly wanted to be with you. And so, with rare exceptions, the relationships I entered were with women who pursued me or let me know in some way that they wanted to be pursued. (I would sometimes pick up on these cues years after the fact.)

Now here was Liz. Even I understood that you don't track someone down at his office, with only a first name and company name to go on, if you're not interested in him romantically, and it was clear that I could become involved with her; the only question was whether or not I wanted to. The evening to come would determine that, since I knew very little about Liz, except that she seemed nice and interesting—and creative, from the sound of things. Some of it, much of it, for better or worse, would depend on physical attraction. I didn't know whether I was attracted to her or not, because at the diner I had barely paid attention to how she looked. I didn't recall thinking she was unattractive, which seemed a good sign—good enough for my mind to begin to construct a woman I hadn't actually seen. As I got off the subway downtown and walked in the winter air to Liz's building, then up to her apartment, I felt optimistic. And then she opened her door, and I got a lesson in how easy it is to con yourself.

The evening was pleasant—more than pleasant in some ways, which I'll get to—but I knew instantly that I would not become romantically involved with Liz. But I was here, we had the evening ahead of us, why not make the most of it?—and maybe we could be friends. She had a comfortable home, the most memorable feature of which was smack in the middle of her living room: a playground-style slide. (I must have gone down it.) Here, I thought, is someone with a great childlike spirit.

In a way, that spirit—the desire to transcend age—became the theme of our acquaintance. It came out that evening that, at thirty-seven, Liz was twelve-plus years older than I was. "I thought you were about thirty-two," she told me. (Months after that evening, I recalled that line to another woman I was involved with briefly. "I'll laugh later," she said.) But our age difference didn't matter to Liz. As for the difference between our skin colors, it didn't even come up, that night or ever, which impresses me in retrospect. We talked about writing; she had published a novel, which I dreamed of doing, and she gave me a copy—"It's good to have copies of your book to give people," she said, "for when it goes out of print." Though she didn't go into it much, I took in that she was involved in theater. At one point we stretched out on her floor to watch TV. She nudged me with her stockinged foot, and we held hands—I remember that she wore dark red polish on elegantly shaped nails; there was enough erotic tension that we rubbed the backs of our hands together, but not enough for me to proceed from there. At the end of the evening, when I put on my coat and stood at her door, she wrapped my scarf, smiling with her prominent front teeth, and gave me a light peck on the lips. She looked hopeful. That makes me sad now.

It is easy for someone my age to forget, and difficult for younger people to understand, how different life was before the internet. Had there been universal access to the World Wide Web in 1988, I could have googled the name on the cover of Liz's novel—Elizabeth Swados—and discovered a few things. She probably told me herself, and I'm sure I asked, where she grew up (Buffalo) and went to school (Bennington College). What she didn't mention, and what I might have found out on the Web in a different era, is that while she was still studying music and writing at Bennington, she met Ellen Stewart, founder of the experimental La MaMa theater in New York; that through La MaMa she met the director Andrei Serban; and that, working with Serban and others, she broke new ground in musical theater. I might have learned that in the late 1970s, when I was a miserable, oblivious junior high school student in D.C., Liz's Broadway show *Runaways*, and Liz herself, were racking up Tony Award nominations.

So, yes—she was, in her way, quite famous. There was more, though. "I recall thinking that this woman was good with kids,"

I wrote in the first paragraph of this essay. I didn't know the half of it. *Runaways* is a series of sung monologues by teen characters who have fled their broken family lives. As research for the show, Liz interviewed numerous hard-luck young people—and then cast them. Others of her works, such as *The Hating Pot*, would take on themes of racism and antisemitism. (Liz was Jewish.) This was the profoundly talented, open-hearted, special person I had taken one look at when, to put it plainly, I thought, *Nah*.

We got together again. I went to her apartment, and from there we went walking. There was, that evening, the feeling of the Village, maybe all of Manhattan, being her playground. We went to a place that was having a dance party—possibly La MaMa, because Liz pointed out Ellen Stewart, who was floating around the huge room like a giant bee. I must have indicated that I didn't know who she was, because Liz said, "Don't tell her that. She'll kill you." Liz introduced me to a man—white, fortyish, good-looking, wearing a blue suit—whose name and possibly very important occupation I have forgotten; I do recall that he smiled at me in a friendly way while his eyes asked: What is *she* doing with *you*? Later we went back to Liz's place. We talked—mostly, she talked, about our age difference, which she seemed to think was holding me back from getting involved with her, and whose unimportance she tried hard to impress upon me. "I had a relationship with a man who was sixty-nine years old," she told me. "He was one of the greatest men I've ever known. Age doesn't matter. What matters is what people are like inside. There are some people you meet, sometimes they're young people, and they're walking around, but it's like they're already *dead*." I had little to say. What she was saying was true, but it missed the point, and I didn't know how to tell her what the point was without hurting her.

What I've learned about Liz since that evening has led me to reflect on the possible significance, for her, of the word "dead."

The book of hers that she gave me a copy of is *Leah and Lazar*, a novel published in 1982. Her nonfiction book *The Four of Us: A*

Family Memoir came out in 1991. I don't know what became of my original copy of *Leah and Lazar*, but I acquired and read both of those books recently. The memoir has four sections, one for each member of Liz's quintessentially dysfunctional immediate family. The first section is about Liz's older brother, Lincoln, a highly creative schizophrenic who was Liz's chief tormentor and the biggest influence on her life, a doomed soul who was disabled after throwing himself in front of a subway train and who later became a street person, dying in a hovel in 1989. The second section tells the story of Liz's mother, a depressed woman of unrealized artistic gifts who killed herself when Liz was a young woman. Next up is Liz's father, a lawyer who brought big-league hockey to Buffalo, a bellicose man with contempt for those—e.g., his wife and son—who gave up on their own lives and who identified himself and his daughter as survivors. Finally, there is Liz herself, whose youthful adventures included living among coal miners in Appalachia, teaching in an African village, traveling as a musician (she once performed with Pete Seeger), and appearing on soap operas (all the ones my grandmother watched—I probably saw her on TV at some point). *Leah and Lazar* was a fictionalized version of all this, remarkable, among other reasons, for telling the story of the death of the brother (Lazar in the novel) with alarming accuracy, seven years before the fact. One part of the novel seems to have been influenced by the research for *Runaways*: the Liz character, Leah, becomes a teen sex worker in Florida before returning to her rather blasé parents. But in a figurative sense, that section of *Leah and Lazar* is perhaps autobiographical. Liz was a runaway from the spirit of death in her family. A refugee, a survivor. Defiantly alive.

One evening, the last one we spent together, Liz and I went to the movies. We saw *Moonstruck*, a romantic comedy in which the Cher character falls in love with her fiancé's brother, played by Nicolas Cage. It was not lost on me that I was a twenty-four-year-old man sitting with a thirty-seven-year-old woman as we watched the twenty-four-year-old Cage declare his love for the forty-one-year-old Cher. Afterward, as we walked to Liz's place, I hummed or whistled part of *Moonstruck*'s soundtrack, which I dimly recalled having heard before but couldn't place, and asked Liz about it. Even then I could feel what she must have been thinking when she looked at me: *He really is young.* "It's from Puccini's opera *La Bohème*," she said evenly.

Our conversation at her apartment was listless, dismal. I don't recall what we said, because it was trivial, and because Liz's tone made our exchange like a dubbed film—her lips were saying one thing, but I heard something else: *I've tried. I'm obviously not going to persuade you. I don't know what else there is to say.* Before long, I left. I never saw or spoke to Liz again.

Unless you count this: one day more than two decades later, in the early 2010s, when I was spending, as usual, way too much time on Facebook, I found Liz's profile. I sent her a friend request. She accepted. There was no exchange beyond that. I don't know if she even remembered who I was, and for my part, I wouldn't have been sure what to write. (*Hi, twenty-odd years ago you wanted us to be lovers, but I wasn't interested. How's it going?*) You might ask why I looked her up at all. It's a good question, one I've asked myself, particularly since early 2016, when I saw the news of Liz's death. Complications after surgery for esophageal cancer. A month short of her sixty-fifth birthday.

How well Liz is remembered depends on whom you're talking to. I recently mentioned her to two well-educated friends, both men, one several years older than I am, the other nine years younger; both immediately thought of the writer Harvey Swados—was Liz his wife? Daughter? (He was a cousin.) On the other hand, the *New York Times* ran a substantial obituary of her (which mentioned, among many other things, that she was survived by her wife) and months later published remembrances of Liz by figures including Meryl Streep.

When I remember Liz—and maybe this has something to do with the Facebook friend request—I think of what she said about some people already being dead. What Liz thought of me is ultimately, of course, both unknowable and unimportant, but I do wonder if she considered me one of those walking dead folks because, as she must have thought, I deferred to societal mores about age differences. What *is* important is what I think of myself, and I realize that over the years I have used Liz's words as a kind of personal yardstick. Have I lived as an alive person? Writing is the one thing I have always pursued whether I knew anyone was interested or not. That fickle, elusive object of affection has nonetheless taken me to some interesting places. (Some of them are Liz's old haunts. I've taught nonfiction writing at Bennington, where she was a student, and NYU, where she was a professor.) I have written steadily; I write because I can't imagine not doing it, because I need to. But one also needs to make a living, and I spent a couple of decades doing work few would describe as glamorous to support myself and the family I always wanted. Would an alive person have done it differently? Would he have put writing front and center, always, until he either hit it big or died the death of Lazar? Looking at these questions written in my notebook, I think I have the beginnings of an answer; but maybe that is less important than asking the question—not about what we've done, but what we're doing.

It is tempting for a human being, especially a writer, and most especially an essayist, to find cause and effect between one event and subsequent events, and if you're not careful you can end up with an essay that might as well be a short story. So I will simply list some things that happened after I last saw Liz.

That spring, my office had a dance party. I asked a coworker to dance (the one who said "I'll laugh later"), and as we were dancing, I asked if she wanted to have coffee after the party. We went from Midtown to a diner in the Village. When we left there and were about to part for the evening, I kissed her. I didn't know if she wanted me to or not. Turned out she liked it.

Four years after that, I married a (different) woman I love deeply and am still with. We've told our daughters the story of our courtship, which at first seemed anything but that. They laugh at how we had to overcome our first impressions, or non-impressions, of each other. "Love at fiftieth sight," our older daughter said once.

One thing that settling down is good for is establishing routines. One of mine is going to the Y. Between that and the fact that, lately, my metabolism appears to have been run over by an eighteen-wheeler, my little body has gotten a bit bigger. Some of that, though not a lot, has made its way down to my legs. I wear shorts and swimming trunks now without a thought. You could call this confidence, or you could say I no longer care, or you could conclude that often the two amount to the same thing.

The other day I listened to a recording of *La Bohème* with Maria Callas singing the part of the fatally ill Mimi. The passage of the music included in *Moonstruck* is actually a very small part of the opera. But it is lovely, and a little sad, and memorable, and once in a while it goes through my head.

New York in Two Reels

ON FILM,

TV, WRITING,

AND HOME

1. SUNDAY IN NEW YORK

At this writing, I have called New York City home for over three decades—years longer than I'd been alive when I moved here. I have lived in Harlem though mostly in my current home of Brooklyn, and I've worked in Manhattan, the Bronx, and Queens. I got married in Prospect Park and sent my children to public schools in Brooklyn and Manhattan. I have served on two juries, voted in nine mayoral elections, and watched the progression from one-dollar subway token to $2.90 MetroCard. I am a New Yorker.

Or am I? I ask this because I wonder whether, if I were truly convinced of and secure in my New Yorkerness, I would still feel the urge that comes over me once a week—on Sundays. I have not seen all of the United States, but I've seen enough to know that much of it shuts down on that day. Not my town, though. That, to me, is the mark of a vibrant city, and there is no better time to be in one than Sunday. You can appreciate what's around you in a way that isn't possible when you're rushing to get to work on time or hurrying to lunch with a client. Gone by Sunday, too, is Saturday's frenzy of celebration. Still at leisure, but with our feet back on the ground, we can take in a city that has slowed down just enough to be seen. This balance of our awareness, the city's magnificence, and its— and our—unhurried pace is a magic formula, making it possible to revel in our New Yorkerness, to do that quintessential *thing* that lets us feel a part of this place. The urge I have on Sundays is to do that thing, my only question being—and I've been here thirty-eight years—*What is it?* A classic movie at Film Forum, or a Yankees game, or a visit to the Brooklyn Museum, or brunch at Sylvia's, or lunch at Katz's Delicatessen, or a ride on the Staten Island Ferry, or a tour of Louis Armstrong's house? I have enjoyed all these things, but the problem with doing anything at all, in any place at any time, is that that thing precludes everything else, which won't cut it if the point is to feel of a piece with a city whose essence is unlimited possibility.

On a recent Sunday, in search of an answer, I turned to a movie from the early 1960s. As with many other movies, I had seen part of it on TV when I was a boy; I had retained very little beyond its title, but this particular title alone had led me to search for it online over the years, always finding it unavailable—until recently. Finally, I had in my hands the work that would yield, if anything could, the secret to capturing the feeling I was after. What better way, after all, than to spend part of a Sunday in New York watching a movie called *Sunday in New York?* When it was over I felt, if I may be permitted a comparison to another film, a bit like Dorothy after she sees the man behind the curtain. *Sunday in New York* is a very enjoyable sex farce that is nonetheless dated by the very thing that must have once made it seem so fresh: the burning question of whether a "girl" should or is expected to bed the guy she's out with. Unlike many works whose day has passed, this one gave me the brief, sad feeling that mine had, too, and not just because the movie was released in the year of my birth. When the twenty-two-year-old Jane Fonda character referred to her parents back in Albany, I realized that those obviously settled folks, not important enough in the movie even to appear on screen, were probably younger than me. More pertinently, this sweet love story, while set in New York on a Sunday, is not about Sunday in New York; shots of rowing in Central Park aside, the setting could be Chicago or San Francisco. I liked the movie, but it didn't have much to tell me.

I was on my own, back to my original question. It might help, as they used to say where I'm from, to break it down. What are the elements of this quintessential New York feeling or experience? What are the things that say "New York" to me? Literature—elegant sentences or verse by the writers, so many writers, who have come here; music—strains from the meeting place of jazz and symphony, grand but playful and unpredictable like the city, works by Duke Ellington, say, or George Gershwin, or Charles Mingus; people— seeing so many walking this way and that. On another Sunday a while back, I tried for some of this. At home I had *The Symphonic Ellington* playing while I read Auden poems, works that are themselves like the city, beautiful and elusive; from time to time I looked out my living room window at bare tree limbs silhouetted against the gray-blue winter sky. After a while I took the Auden collection with me to a diner down the street, where I read while sipping black coffee and watching strangers go by the window. I thoroughly enjoyed myself, though eventually something occurred to me about this afternoon of experiencing New York: I had barely left home.

But maybe, if this quintessential New York experience can be even partly achieved in one's living room, it is largely a state of mind. And maybe any New York activity, incomplete though it may be, is the real deal for that very reason: its incompleteness proves you're in the right place. You can take in all of Hudson, New York, in an afternoon. Not so New York City. You get there only a piece at a time, and you never get there. And if you did, what then? Would they let you ride the subway for free? The frustrating thing about New York is also what makes it oddly comforting: you can't do everything there is to do, any more than you can read every book ever published or watch every film ever released—which means you will never run out. For the completists among us, it may be better to think of each little piece as a DNA sample, making do for the whole. Maybe you live here; maybe you visited once; either way, you've had part of the experience. I will try to remember this on some Sunday while looking down the long, long stretch of Park Avenue as I walk along in the East 80s, on my way to the Metropolitan Museum of Art . . .

2. NAKED CITY

For a time in the late 1980s, a local TV station in New York City aired late-night reruns of *Naked City*. The show, a black-and-white police drama set in New York, had originally aired from 1958 to 1963, the year of my birth. Those years were a critical period in the civil rights movement, and, in its quiet way, *Naked City* reflected that. The show's regular cast—playing a squad of detectives—was as white as the cast of every other show of the era, and so were most if not all of its guest stars, but in small parts, not all of them speaking roles, Blacks had begun to pop up here and there. It wasn't much in itself. It was a start, in what seemed a new day.

I had gotten my own start in New York in the mid-1980s, popping up as one of very few Black faces at a book publishing company. At around the time the *Naked City* reruns began, I had come to a crossroads at the company; I could stay or I could go, and I decided to go, electing to do just enough brain-deadening part-time data-entry work to support me while I focused on writing.

Is there a limit to how nostalgic a person ought to feel, or to how many things he ought to feel that way about? I have nostalgia for this period of my life. I was young, twenty-five years old, and immersed in writing. At the time, I felt the same way, if that is possible, toward a New York I never knew, the one represented on *Naked City*. Nostalgia is a purifying vision, one that removes complication. When I think of hanging out and writing in my apartment in the emphatically unfashionable Cypress Hills section of Brooklyn, for example, I do not focus on how lonely I sometimes was, or on the mice that had the run of the place, or on the soul-killingly long subway ride to Manhattan. And when I think of the era during which *Naked City* was made, I tend not to remember that I wouldn't have been allowed to vote in certain parts of the country then, or that if a Black person was mentioned as a potential presidential candidate, a punch line was coming.

The black-and-white photographs of a Ukrainian-born New Yorker named Usher Fellig, known popularly as Weegee, inspired the 1948 film *The Naked City*, directed by the noir specialist Jules Dassin. Weegee got wind of murders by hanging around police headquarters in Manhattan and being the only photographer with a portable police-band shortwave radio, which he closely monitored. He often beat cops to crime scenes and sold his pictures to newspapers. His shots of bodies left bleeding on sidewalks and of other, happier slices of the city—rapt listeners at a jazz club, kids playing in front of a turned-on fire hydrant on a sunlit street in summer—reflected the everyday exoticism of New York.

Dassin and company brought a similar spirit to the film, which was shot on location; various sequences show the Staten Island Ferry, zoom in on passengers riding a crowded subway train, and follow characters to their homes in the outer boroughs. The particulars that *The Naked City* records—the ubiquity of fedoras, the supremacy of print journalism—are long gone, but the essence of a New York captured in the film is timeless.

A decade after the film's release came the television show it inspired, also shot in black and white, many of its episodes featuring the serious, laconic detective Adam Flint and his world-weary yet good-humored superiors, dressed, like Adam, in fedoras and raincoats. Often running afoul of the detectives are the many characters who pass through the episodes of *Naked City*, trying desperately to escape the consequences of their bad, irrevocable decisions, their pale foreheads glistening with sweat as hindsight sharpens their regret to the fineness of a needle. Behind them, meanwhile, silent witness to their desperation, to their worst and best intentions, is the physical city, its buildings, rising above the bare limbs of trees in Central Park, a backdrop to the characters' fleeting lives. If wisdom comes too late to those characters, if they are doomed, the world they inhabit seems to me eternal. The reason it seems so is the same reason that the television show triggers nostalgia in me while the movie that inspired it, made a decade earlier, does not; and in my response is the key to a certain brand of nostalgia. To visit a world as it was fifteen or twenty years before our birth is to go to a foreign land; but to visit that same world at the moment of our debut—in my case the early 1960s, when the TV show was made—is to hit the reset button, to a time when our lives were all future and no past, when the inevitable random turns in our journey had not yet closed off other routes, when anything, everything, was possible. The promises we have made to ourselves, the promises the world has made to us, have not yet been betrayed. This long-ago world is eternally new.

On a Saturday in January 1989, in a new brown leather jacket and new hat—not a fedora but a gray newsboy-style cap—I boarded a bus from New York's Port Authority to Harrisburg, Pennsylvania, to do research for a novel I was writing. In Harrisburg I walked around the perfectly serviceable downtown, which to a New Yorker—even a transplanted one like me—seemed dinky and pathetic; one detail of Harrisburg I have retained is the clothing store under whose name were the words "Fine Clothing Since 1972." There was a bar-restaurant I went to in the late afternoon, where I fell into a conversation with a guy who told me about his adventures as a cop and as the road manager (or something) for the music group Menudo. And then I boarded the bus back to New York. This was the period when I was immersed in *Naked City*, with its gorgeous shots of the city as it looked when I was born. It was dark when my bus approached the city, and there it was, that famous bright skyline. Deep in the bowels of Port Authority, the other sleepy passengers and I disembarked, each of us to his or her own life and possibilities. Could I make myself into a writer? I didn't know, as I got on the downtown A train and headed deep into Brooklyn, that the question would bring not so much a yes or no answer as a life—with the city as a silent witness—in which I struggled to make sense of notions of Blackness and whiteness, to understand my own and other people's motivations and intentions, bad and good, and to make good use of my own fleeting time.

Interlude

ON FILM

AND ROMANCE

In 1989 the change from summer to fall occurred on Saturday, September 23, in the early afternoon. That is when Amy Peck and I, Amy wearing a sleeveless yellow top, crossed a street in Greenwich Village, on our way to see *Dr. Strangelove*, and felt the temperature drop.

I had first heard Amy's name six years earlier, also in September. I had just arrived in London, for my junior-year college semester abroad, and was milling about with my classmates in the room where we were to have so many discussions of the plays we saw. On that first day I introduced myself to Charles Hawley, who was to become my lifelong friend, or he introduced himself to me; and as we stood there, or so my memory has it, Charles told me about the woman who had, the year before, broken his heart.

We had returned to our college campus in the States when, one January day, I crossed the snow-covered quad to Charles's tiny single dorm room. That was my introduction to Amy, who had short blond hair and sat on the edge of the bed with her hands in the pockets of her black overcoat. She and Charles decided to "work on a good solid friendship," in the phrase Charles used more than once.

Amy and Charles graduated that spring. Two years later, after graduating, having my own heart broken, and moving—for reasons not unrelated—to New York, I saw Amy one morning on the subway. We chatted. Much later, I asked her what she had thought of me that day. "I thought you seemed nervous," she said.

That forthrightness was there from the beginning. Late on a Sunday afternoon in 1989, while living in Harlem, I saw that *Lawrence of Arabia* was playing downtown (most of Manhattan is downtown when you live on 150th Street) and called around for people to see it with later in the evening. That took a while. Before finding someone to go with me (the poet Jena Osman, another London-semester friend), I tried Amy, whose number Charles had once given me. Amy, who lived in Brooklyn, was comfortably settled in at home on that Sunday evening and was reluctant to hop on the subway to the Upper West Side at the last minute to see a four-hour film; or, as she put it when I called her, "Are you crazy?"

Crazy or not, I had entered her mind as someone she might see movies with. That was how, a few months later, we saw a strange film Amy had read about, *The Navigator*. Amy assumed that when it was over we would go our separate ways. I assumed we would get something to eat. We got something to eat. And our meal at Pizzeria Uno on Sixth Avenue in the Village is where it began to happen. Amy felt comfortable enough to begin talking about her childhood, including visits to her grandmother's house in D.C., where she and her sister and brother, those three young New Yorkers, collected acorns in the front yard.

We did more things together, I and this slender woman with the unusually wide yet narrow eyes, with the warmth just below the acerbic top layer. In a bar in the Village on the night of that Saturday in September, I was talking with sadness in my voice about my very old grandmother when Amy touched my forearm.

But that was hours ahead as we crossed the street on the way to *Dr. Strangelove* and felt the temperature fall. So much falling on that September day.

Out of the Past

ON FAMILY,

WORK, AND

LOOKING BACK

My first memory of the place is of seeing four Black women sitting at a cluster of adjoined desks. The sight surprised me. I had seen similar ones at editorial offices before, but only at those of African American publications, a category that did not include *Current Biography*. The sight also made me feel at home. These women, past thirty (two were well past it), reminded me of my aunts. This was not the usual job-hunting experience at a Midtown Manhattan publishing company. But then, this was not the usual publishing company. And we were quite a ways north of Midtown Manhattan.

That is not to say that the H. W. Wilson Company, situated in the South Bronx on the banks of the Harlem River, a few minutes' walk from Yankee Stadium, was progressive or hip. Hipness and progressivism, in fact, had they somehow stumbled onto this place, would have found their opposites amid the long, long hallways of dull brown carpeting, the tomblike quiet, and the stacks upon stacks of magazines whose contents were read, summarized, and listed alphabetically by subject in the volumes of *Readers' Guide to Periodical Literature*, *Book Review Digest*, and many other indexes compiled here at this outpost of the library world, the workplace of those who were not up for the excitement of the library.

Well, that's being reductive—not to mention mean. Wilson may not have completely transcended the stereotype of the frumpy, nerdy librarian; but there is treasure to be found in most places if you're of a mind to look, and many at Wilson, besides being book-smart, were also thoughtful and personable with good senses of humor. And if most of Wilson's publications were not ones that anybody would read at length, there was also *Current Biography*.

H. W. Wilson had been around for forty-two years when, in 1940, the first green, hardbound volume of *Current Biography* appeared. (The language of *CB*'s early articles reflected the times in which they were written. The entry on Joe Louis, for example, referred to the legendary heavyweight boxing champion as "this big Negro boy.") And *CB* had been around for fifty-two years when, in late 1992, I first wended my way past my faux aunts to the office of the editor (which, half a dozen years later, would be my office). Aside from the women I first saw, *CB*'s staff on the day of my interview was, in fact, not Black. The editor, Judith Graham, whom we called Jennie, a tall, well-educated, moody, faded beauty of a woman, was in her early fifties then; the thin, blond, driven Liz, the senior editor and second-in-command, was my age (twenty-nine); two of the associate editors, the brainy blond bombshell Hilary and the tall, long-haired, gruff southerner Gray, were, respectively, one and two years younger than me; and the third, the quiet, eagle-eyed Miriam, who would later become my friend and right hand, in effect my coeditor, was forty-eight. I joined the staff in January 1993 as the copyeditor, and after exactly a year I was an associate editor, too, working on articles submitted by freelancers and writing more and more of them myself. Years later, when Wilson had become as corporatized and numbers-driven as such a place could get, when *CB* had done away with its longtime stable of freelancers in favor of a revolving door of miserably paid young full-time staff writers, I would ride herd over pages of sometimes execrable prose; but in those sleepy days of my first years at Wilson, I found myself, for the first time in my life, truly at home in a workplace, one among equals, holding a mug of coffee while standing with Jennie beside Miriam's or Hilary's cubicle to discuss the finer points of grammar or whether my use of "reminiscent of" was quite right.

CB depended for most of its information on secondary sources—articles from newspapers and magazines, many of which, in turn, relied on *CB*—which is where my faux aunts came in. In those last pre-internet days, Carolyn, Rhonda, Madelyn, and Ethel spent their time clipping articles on people in the news. (During the year I was the copyeditor, my desk was next to that of one of the two older women, Ethel, who was—in the sweetest, most wonderful way—daft; the other, Carolyn, whom I also loved and who loved me, would later work under me, playing the longtime drill sergeant to my young officer—giving me a hard time, for example, about how messy my office was. For reasons that were never clear to me, Carolyn was not on speaking terms with the other three. Those were not the only fraught relationships in the office.) The four women placed the clippings in the tan file drawers that surrounded our offices, alphabetizing them by subject. After we associate editors pitched ideas to Jennie for people to profile in *CB*, the first stop was the file drawer, and if there was a nice, fat pile of clippings on, say, Stan Lee (my first pitch, and the first, unsigned *CB* article I wrote as a staff member), Jennie would give the OK, and a *CB* article was conceived.

To think of that time now is to perform the temporal equivalent of gazing across a continental divide. I can see everything clearly; and I can't get there from here.

Life was sleepier then in other ways too. As I write this, the end of the summer of 2017 approaches, and if the country and the world are not actually coming apart, they are putting on an awfully convincing show. By contrast, I began my career at Wilson five days after Bill Clinton, the first Democratic president in a dozen years, took the oath of office, and for many of us it was a hopeful time. Like the country, I was making a transition. In the way of some who aspire to literary prose, I had spent four-plus years—which corresponded roughly to the presidency of George Herbert Walker Bush—working part-time and making a short-lived attempt at being an expatriate, all while writing, but now I was returning to full-time work. Less than a year earlier, I had gotten married. I was bringing a period of professional and romantic wandering to a close, exchanging it for novel domesticity, and, as if to apply an exclamation point to that idea, my thirtieth birthday brought the news that we would have a baby.

"Sleepy" is both an accurate description and an ironic one, since the thing I did least following my little girl's arrival was sleep. My main memory of new fatherhood is of settling on the couch in those other-worldly hours beyond night and too dark for morning, with my daughter nestled in the crook of my arm, drinking from the bottle I had groggily fixed for her, as I watched TV—abysmal made-for-television movies from my own childhood in the 1970s, as if that quiet, dark, no-man's-hour provided a portal to an earlier era.

There were other such portals. I used to joke that, given Wilson's stodginess, working there was like taking a train each day to the 1950s. My subway commute to the South Bronx was an hour and fifteen minutes door-to-door; I took to wearing fedoras in those days, and not only did I imagine that I was a more urban, darker-skinned version of the daily commuters in the world of John Cheever's stories: I was steeping in other fictional worlds too. As I began to build a family and career—to foster my child's life, to assemble my own—I tried to extend the ragged ends of the literary education I had acquired so lackadaisically in college, bringing more serious consideration to the books I now read on the train. And at lunch, at a cubicle near a window with a view of the muddy waters of the Harlem River, I took a crack at creating literature myself, writing (in longhand) fiction that never saw the light of day, essays that began to.

Most of my day, though, was spent in a kind of introvert's dream. With dozens of clippings scattered about my desk, articles that occasionally *did* go back to the 1950s and provided many pieces of my subjects' lives, I began to assemble those lives as well. Some of the subjects were foreign politicians, and I read about their systems of government; some were writers, and I read what they told interviewers about craft. Some were businesspeople, some boxers, some musicians. I synthesized what I learned into three-thousand-word articles in anonymous prose as original and elegant as I knew how to make it, getting better at technical aspects of writing in the only way there is to improve at anything: doing it. I typed on a computer that was not yet hooked up to the internet, that provided none of today's constant distractions, that merely stored what I wrote. I got lost in my work in a way that feels impossible now.

Where is the past? Some physicists believe that it is an actual place, located in a dimension not separate from those we currently occupy, that it is mathematically and theoretically though not practically possible to get to—the journey being dependent on "exotic matter" we don't yet know about and being subject, in addition, to all kinds of unpredictable problems. There are other ways to reach the past, of course, but those can also present difficulties, not in arriving but in getting back again. In the many years since I turned thirty, I have discovered how easy it is—my two now-grown children will vouch for this—to get stuck in the "Things aren't what they used to be" mode.

Maybe a better question is: *What* is the past? According to the celebrated first line of L. P. Hartley's 1953 novel, *The Go-Between*, "The past is a foreign country: they do things differently there." But the past is also a fictional world, almost the way Hartley's novel or one of Cheever's stories is fictional, made up of elements that resemble our actual lives but aren't quite the same. The past resides in memory, of course, and yet memory is a kind of smudged funhouse mirror, enlarging some things, shrinking others, hiding still others completely. For example: the golden haze with which my memory imbues my time at Wilson tends to obscure the number of occasions, while I was there, on which I thought of leaving. For a publishing outfit, Wilson was off the beaten path, geographically (its mostly Black and Hispanic neighborhood, I eventually discovered, was in the poorest congressional district in the United States) and in other ways too. Jennie, my old boss, who had a way of confiding in me—a confidence I hope I am not betraying too badly here—once told me of fantasizing that she would wake up one morning and discover that her twenty-odd years at *CB* had been a dream, that she had not, as she seemed to feel she had, wasted her career, if not her life. I spent a number of years at Wilson that I would describe today as happy and fulfilling, yet I recall being unsurprised, if a bit hurt, the time I met with an editorial headhunter, a woman who looked at my résumé and asked about my years at the company, "What did you do, take a wrong turn?" My going to a headhunter seems to indicate that I was not completely happy; but if the head-hunter hadn't asked that tactless question, it's altogether possible that I would have forgotten I went to her.

I sometimes find myself pitying people of the distant past, with their limited knowledge and technology, their tendency, so easy to see in retrospect, to worry needlessly over some things (Y2K) and be blindsided by others (9/11). No doubt someone not yet born will one day pity me the same way. Perhaps classic literature is, among many other things, a corrective to this idea. I can pity the people of, say, the early 1950s as much as I like, and yet a passage in a book from that time—"The past is never dead. It's not even past"—is as insightful as anything likely to be written or spoken today or in the future.

In 1995, from my desk at *CB*, I sent my first-ever email, to my old college friend Tracy. I was amazed when I got a reply. This thing actually worked! The internet had arrived. Among its many other ramifications, the job of clipping newspaper and magazine articles became obsolete. Two of the women who had done it, Carolyn and Rhonda, were soon reassigned. Ethel and Madelyn were let go. This was part of a larger shakeup at *CB*. Some of us survived, and a few did not; no one was unaffected, and my happiest years at the company, when I could spend my days learning about the world and honing my writing skills without a manager's headaches, came to an end. Some years later, Wilson itself was sold to a company head-quartered far away, and most of us lost our jobs. These were times, for me, when yesterday suddenly came to seem like the distant past. There have been other such times, much more dramatic ones, not just for me but for most people I know, one of them in 2016.

The past—the time of my faux aunts, say, or, going back even further, my real aunts—has at least one thing going for it. We know that things are not what they were, and that we are not who we were. In this way, the past, wherever and whatever it is, lets us know that the way things are is not the way they will always be.

Blues for Mister Stanley

ON CRITICISM,

RACE, AND

IDENTITY

I met Stanley Crouch in 1994. He was nearing fifty, stocky, balding, at or close to the peak of his fame and his bull-like force. *Notes of a Hanging Judge* (1990), the first of his five essay collections, had cemented his reputation as a cultural critic, and among other major awards, he had received the MacArthur Foundation's Genius Grant. With the trumpeter Wynton Marsalis and the writer Albert Murray, he had cofounded Jazz at Lincoln Center, a living monument to the music he loved and championed so fiercely.

At the time I was a thirty-one-year-old associate editor at *Current Biography*. I wrote a profile of Stanley for *CB*, largely as an excuse to bond with the man whose work had given me answers to questions I hadn't fully formed. To a limited extent, it worked: we kept in occasional touch, and I was once a guest at a Jazz at Lincoln Center concert, seated between Stanley and Murray as they traded observations across my lap. But the most memorable thing Stanley communicated to me during those years came to me through my wife. She and Stanley met briefly at the memorial service for Roger Straus of the book publishing house Farrar, Straus & Giroux, where my wife (like her father) had once worked; my wife told Stanley she was married to me. He told her, "Oh yeah, Cliff. He's a friend—but he's too respectful. Tell him to do something about that."

Since Stanley's death, at seventy-four, on September 16, 2020, I've thought about that remark and how it represents what was best and worst in his public persona. That persona helped save me. Those questions I had not fully formed: What does it mean to be a Black American? What attitude do you take toward the only home you've ever known, one built on the degradation of people who looked like you? How do you love that home without hating yourself? How do you express your defiance, the way Black nationalists did, without leaving yourself, in a sense, homeless? The answer—growled to me from between the lines of Stanley's prose—was that you do it by claiming your American birthright with the fury and acid of the most furious and acidic of America-damning Black separatists. You do it, particularly if you're Stanley, by both insisting on the interrelation of all Americans *and* celebrating Black people's special contributions to America; you do it, particularly if you're Stanley, by setting jazz as the bar of Black American excellence, grit, and imagination; and you do it, most particularly if you're Stanley, by shooting to kill in encounters with those who think differently. My reluctance to do that last part probably explains Stanley's comment about me, and Stanley's refusal to do anything else made his heroism inseparable from his villainy.

Stanley's ideas, in the main, came from Murray, whose dozen books include the 1970 essay collection *The Omni-Americans*. But Stanley might be said to have been the Malcolm X to Murray's Elijah Muhammad, the fiery disciple who spread his mentor's ideas farther than the mentor himself. Oh, how all four men would have hated that comparison. But I will (disrespectfully!) extend it long enough to add that Stanley, like Malcolm, was an exciting figure to some for the same reason that he angered others. I used the word "villainy" above, but a more accurate word may be "fanaticism," bright and shining with its dark flip side of intolerance. Stanley's modus operandi as a cultural critic, for good or ill, was to find fault with the part and then take a shotgun to the whole. So rap music, that self-expression of the marginalized, some of which has very unfortunate leanings toward misogyny and romanticizes the "gangsta" life, was *all* worthless in Stanley's view, a celebration of the worst aspects of Black life. Rock music was to Stanley the inexplicably adored idiot grandchild of the blues, besmirching the family name. Toni Morrison's novels, in which Stanley perceived a Black wallowing in victimhood, were "bottles of bathtub corn liquor" given "high-class seals" (a line that drew an audible gasp at the public reading where I first met Stanley face-to-face). Spike Lee was a "nappy-headed Napoleon," Miles Davis's spearheading of jazz-rock fusion made him a "sellout," and on and on. Some hated Stanley's dismissiveness, but it got attention of the kind that nuance and ambivalence seldom do; its sound was sharp enough to pierce the din and then, in the brief, rare, bewildered silence that followed, say something coherent.

Because Stanley's targets were often Black, many called him a tool of The (white) Man. But it always seemed to me that there was much more to it than that. If he overreached, he was sincere; his attitudes were hard-won and deeply held, reflections of an unusual personal journey in that deeply strange land called America.

He was born in late 1945 in Los Angeles. His father, a drug addict, was mostly absent from Stanley's life, but his mother, a maid, inspired him intellectually, exposing him to newspaper editorials, classic films, and jazz. Stanley came of age amid the racial unrest of the 1960s and embraced Black nationalism. He tried his hand at acting and playing drums, published a volume of poems, and taught literature at the Claremont Colleges. He eventually soured on nationalism, feeling, as he once put it, that he "was in a kind of reverse Ku Klux Klan rally," and came under the spell of the more inclusive vision of Murray and Ralph Ellison.

If the Stanley-Malcolm-Murray-Muhammad comparison holds water, an even better one—and I've long suspected that Stanley himself had this in mind—involves James Baldwin and Richard Wright, who along with Ellison and Langston Hughes were the most prominent Black male American writers of the twentieth century. In perhaps American literature's most famous example of biting the hand that feeds you, Baldwin wrote takedowns of Wright, his benefactor, in the essays "Everybody's Protest Novel" and "Alas, Poor Richard." Stanley's version of that was "Some Words about Albert Murray," which included scathing takes on his friend and mentor's novels. That essay, perhaps Stanley's attempt to step out a bit from Murray's shadow, came at a cost. "Stanley's on my *s* list," Murray said to me, and he never got off it.

But it won't do to dwell on Stanley's supposed sins without coming back to his writing. I recently reread his long, beautiful 1983 essay "Body and Soul," reprinted in *Hanging Judge*. Its eighteen parts cover the Umbria Jazz Festival, with ruminations on Italian history, art, and people; someone investigating the subjects of jazz, or Renaissance painting, or both could do worse than to start with this essay. I had forgotten much of it, but the years had not dimmed my memory of one comparison Stanley made: the proto-Renaissance painter Giotto "stripped away what [Kenneth] Clark calls the 'decorative jumble' of images that made the medieval school both highly stylized and emblematic, offering in its place the weight and sacrifice, the disappointment and the exaltation of human beings concurring and conflicting. In a sense, he discovered the individual in the pageant. . . . In his own way, Louis Armstrong did the same. He discovered that his powers of imagination could stand alone, with the clarinet and the trombone of the conventional New Orleans band silenced"—making way for the jazz solo. Later in the essay, he wrote of "relaxing into the thought of how much of my own experience had been clarified by exposure to foreign forms." It would be hard to overstate the effect of those passages on my imagination.

In early 2019 or so came the news that an accident at home had left Stanley in bad shape—and in a nursing home, where he had "lost a step," as someone put it. My friend and fellow writer Adam Shatz suggested that we visit Stanley together. One March day we took a train to the facility in the Riverdale section of the Bronx.

Wending our way up stairs, through halls, and past a lot of art, we came to an open area, a reminder of what awaits so many of us. White-haired, mostly white people sat, mostly in wheelchairs, in various stages of absence, some with mouths hanging open, breathing and staring but showing few other signs of life, bodies whose minds, after a long marriage, had slipped out one day and not come back. In the middle of this gathering was Stanley. When we went up to him, and Adam reminded him of who we were, Stanley smiled and said, "My day just got better."

We followed as a staff member wheeled him to his room. There, Stanley held forth with stories that had trouble coming to a point. But things changed dramatically when the subject turned to jazz. His observations about Ornette Coleman and others were as sharp as ever.

When Adam and I were about to leave, I said to Stanley, "I just want to tell you that I owe you a big debt."

He said, "I don't think anybody owes anybody."

Summer of '07

A lot of people consider the number 7 to be lucky. Not me. I have passed the age of fifty and can't remember a year ending in 7 that I didn't find to be downright wretched, personally speaking. Maybe 1967 was a good year—I couldn't tell you, having been four at the time—but if so, the trend has been downward since then. In 1977 I was fourteen, and . . . you could probably finish that sentence yourself. I was twenty-four in 1987, a year when I was busy proving the old saw about youth being wasted on the young—single, lonely, hating my ill-paying job, living with more mice than I'd ever seen in one place, I imagined that I had something to complain about, or else I imagine now that my troubles at the time were as simple as a lack of confidence and imagination. Ten short (in retrospect) years later, I was thirty-four, married with a three-year-old daughter, and had just begun my life as a manager, a fifteen-year career that, like Mr. Darcy, showed me its disagreeable side before I became acquainted with its charms.

I may be giving the sense that I've had an unhappy life, which is not my intention, and which in any case would be untruthful.

There were, between the years ending in 7, many good times, even a few great ones. It is just that the vehicle of my life, like a plane, has had to descend every so often for refueling, and over the years I've noticed a certain regularity.

The plane seemed almost to crash-land in 2007. I should qualify that. I did not lose my home, my health (though for a while I wondered about that), or even my job. Still, there are times when one's life, while maintaining its outer shape, goes berserk within, like the contents of the aforementioned plane in its too-rapid approach to the ground. There was, to start with, my job as a manager; that summer the built-in turnover rate of my young, woefully underpaid staff accelerated to the point of ridiculousness, and seemingly every forty-eight hours, someone came into my office, closed the door, and tried to contain his or her glee while giving two weeks' notice. I would miss some of those people more than others, but all of them were missed in the sense that there was a monthly publication to put out and every vacancy made the job that much harder. There was my daughter, who was thirteen in 2007 and by that time had a sister; I now understand, because her sister, too, has since entered thirteen and come out the other side, that the emotional chaos of that age can have less to do with the person than with the time of life, but in the summer of 2007 I lacked that soothing perspective. (Thirteen: now there's a number that lives up to its reputation.) Meanwhile, two-hundred-plus miles away, in D.C., my mother, as became increasingly clear that summer, was dying.

Not coincidentally, during that period I had frequent attacks of heartburn, a couple of them so bad that I wondered if I was about to check out too. The gastroenterologist I finally consulted, an agreeably gruff old pro, started by taking my blood pressure, announcing afterward, "You seem calm, but you are not calm." (I later used that line in a graphic novel.) He said something similar after my endoscopy, the procedure in which a tube with a camera attached is put down the patient's throat. (The camera found nothing. The diagnosis was stress.) During the endoscopy I had a dream that I was on a train with my daughters and was trying to tell them something—I don't know what, just as I don't know where the train was going—but somehow I couldn't get the words out. "Mr. Thompson," someone said, bringing me around, and I staggered into the doctor's office and sat next to my wife, listening through the thinning fog of sedation as the doctor told her, "Your husband is a tense man. Even while he was unconscious, he was fighting the tube."

A lot of people think everything happens for a reason. Not me. I'm not saying it isn't true; I simply have no proof one way or the other, and even if that's how things work, I can't see why the grand design would necessarily benefit a sub-speck in the universe like me. But sometimes it helps to take the long view, if not of the universe, then of one's own little life; and once in a great while, it's good to give oneself a break, a truth I sometimes need help remembering. When I look back at my twenty-four-year-old self, for example, I can wish that he'd had a little more confidence and imagination here and there, or I can acknowledge that that skinny kid had possessed enough of both to get himself to New York, where he would find some good things, or they would find him. I can wince at the memory of the mistakes and misfortunes that characterized my first year as a manager, or I can realize that those experiences made me better at what I had taken on, put me in a position to provide better for my family for years to come; and I can remember that all the turnover of a decade later allowed me to build my staff again almost from scratch, applying what I'd learned about hiring to put together the best crew I ever had. (A few years later we all lost our jobs, but that's another matter.) As for my daughters, their stories are not mine to tell, but I will say that they found resources within themselves to get through that dreaded age, and they ought to be proud of that.

On the other hand, I still miss my mother, still imagine I can call the old number and hear her smile as she says, "Well, hello there, Clifford." Sometimes the crap life throws at you is just crap.

You can't always know, in the thick of those unlucky years, those tough ages, whether there is an upside to the pain. (The most recent year ending in 7 brought the inauguration of the forty-fifth president. I am still looking for the silver lining to that particular cloud.) Possibly there is no knowing, only getting through, which is like talking to young daughters while riding a train and suffering some mysterious throat blockage: where you're going is unclear, and what you're trying to do may not seem to be working. But trying is the only chance. Maybe that's what I wanted to tell them.

Eric Garner and Me

ON RACE,

IDENTITY,

AND REDEMPTION

Please permit me a crude analogy. The fall of 2014 was like an unforeseen rainstorm, a cracking open of a heretofore cloudless sky of the kind that occurred on bad sitcoms of years gone by: everyone who was caught unprepared—i.e., everyone—scrambled for the nearest cover, these people heading to that awning, those people to another. The rain, in this analogy, is the non-indictment of the police officers who choked Eric Garner to death, as shown on the videotape seen by the entire world—this, close on the heels of the non-indictment of the police officer who shot Michael Brown to death, and sixteen months after the non-conviction of the self-appointed public guardian who shot and killed Trayvon Martin. The awnings, in this analogy, are our ready-made opinions about it all. From the crowd under one awning: *This is the kind of justice Blacks can expect in a white society, which is no justice at all.* From the other side of the street: *The so-called victims must have been doing something wrong.*

And then there were those of us, few at first glance, caught in the middle of the street. I am not merely trying to seem different or special, like the kid who answers "Present" instead of "Here" when the teacher takes attendance. And I don't mean to suggest that I was neutral in the debate. In fact, I was one of those shutting down traffic on Broadway in New York while chanting, in an echo of Eric Garner's last words, "I can't breathe!" But to stretch this analogy possibly further than it will go, as I went out to protest in the falling rain, the squall blinded me to what I had long believed, perhaps blinded me to the existence of others who, just maybe, were getting drenched along with me.

The unpunished killings of men with skin like mine got me angry enough to voice an unequivocal statement—*This must stop!*—of the kind I seldom seem able to make. I lack ideological cover. For many, that cover is merely being Black; for many, Blackness, like a press secretary, determines their responses to life and events, externally if not internally. My own press secretary has long cowered under his desk, driven there by others' anger at his words, by his own lack of faith in what he says, by his occasional struggle even to form a statement, by new information that would make that statement obsolete.

I am mixing metaphors, usually a sign of confusion, of a need to simplify, step back, breathe deeply, start at the beginning.

Everyone can complain about his childhood, but I have no more complaints than anyone else, and fewer than most. I was cared for, loved. I was raised, though not purposely, to see the world in neutral terms. Our small, semidetached red brick house did not have an abundance of space (in my earliest years I slept in a room with my sisters and my grandmother), but we had a basement and a backyard, where the view of a housing project, in which my friends lived, reminded me that I was not actually poor. It's not that I thought I was rich; rich was what you saw on TV. But seeing that most of the TV-rich were white did not lead me to any conclusions, since not all of the TV whites were rich, and, hell, the Black family on *The Jeffersons* had their own maid. Maybe the twin pillars of the neutrality with which I viewed the world were the things missing from my little corner of it: (1) discussion of white people— my family simply never talked about them; and (2) white people themselves. In those formative years, I had no scarring experiences, in fact very few experiences of any kind, with whites, unless you count my being told, by classmates, that I talked like one. I knew, of course, about slavery, because everyone knew about slavery, but I also knew, or at least sensed, that a new day had come. There were still racists, of course, but racism as the law of the land had ended. Maybe, once, most white people had been evil. But that was over. The clock had been reset.

And so, in the early 1980s—in this new era for which Martin Luther King Jr. had died—when I went away to a rather prestigious, mostly white college, a surprise awaited me, though it wasn't white racism. Instead, when a Black student circulated a pamphlet about the need to address the prejudice and discrimination we Blacks suffered, I honestly did not know what he was talking about. I felt like I had landed in a 3-D movie house where I alone was without glasses. Weren't we all allowed to enroll in the same classes, live in the same dorms? Any segregation, it seemed to me, was voluntary: in the cafeteria, Black students tended to eat together, and many if not most of them lived in African Heritage House, a dorm I had seen listed as I filled out housing forms but had not chosen. That decision did not reflect any disdain; I simply didn't see the need. I was proud of my heritage—as an elementary school student I had turned in *unassigned* reports based on entries in my Afro-American history book—but my pride did not require a whole dorm. So I was assigned to a residence where (another surprise) I turned out to be the only Black male. Not that it bothered me, not particularly. I befriended some of the whites around me; I dated one (for far too long), and then, later, another. Ironically, it was after moving into a different dorm my sophomore year, and making a couple of Black friends, that I learned how much contempt a lot of Black students had for me. And that's when the philosophy my family had implicitly passed on to me hardened into a creed, an emotional armor: I would judge people as individuals, if I had to judge them at all. I would befriend, date, marry whomever I wanted. If you didn't like it, to hell with you.

Let us fast-forward to 2014, when I found myself somehow no longer in my college years but deep in that hazily defined period called middle age. The Brooklyn neighborhood where I have long lived is mostly, like my wife, white. Over the years, as I've gotten farther physically from the Black community (wherever that is), I've come to understand more about what plagues it. There was never a movie-style "Aha!" moment; more a piecemeal gathering of information, a gradual putting-together of a puzzle with a few areas still to be filled in. (I am always suspicious of those who see the puzzle as child's play.) I've learned some things just by walking around with brown skin—getting followed out of stores, having someone call the police after seeing me leave my own residence. I've learned other things from studying history over the decades, such as the southern practice of convict leasing, or arresting men essentially for the crime of being Black and then hiring them out as (unpaid) prison labor until they died, a system that extended slavery, in all but name, into the twentieth century; incidents including the epidemic of lynching and the Tulsa massacre of 1921, in which whites burned the nation's wealthiest Black community to the ground; and the exclusion of Blacks, during the post–World War II boom, from housing loans of the kind that allowed whites to accumulate and pass on property and wealth, which contributes to disparities to this day. All of it adds up to a more detailed version of what I already knew about, what everyone knows about: the terrible abuse Blacks have faced in America, and—allow me to drop the present-perfect tense—continue to *face*, from harsher prison sentencing, to the placing of toxic waste near poor (i.e., Black and Hispanic) neighborhoods, to the congressional stonewalling of the country's first Black president, to things that, no doubt, we aren't even aware of.

And yet what other country do we have? Most of us, for all the kente cloth we like to wear, have never been to Africa. While learning more about Blacks' often miserable experience in these United States, I have learned more, too, about what we've accomplished in spite of it all, which includes giving this nation its sound as well as large parts of its culture. The pride I felt even as a boy reading his Afro-American history book has only grown, and I cannot feel that the Black American story has been a wholly bad one. Through it all—my marriage attests to this—I've maintained my faith, above all else, in assessing people for who they are, not what they look like. It is, simply, *the right thing to do*.

Oh, I get angry. Sometimes I talk to other Blacks who seem to think, though they never come out and say so, that I just don't get it, "it" being the hard kernel at the center of things, the undeniable, fundamental unfairness of our situation, the one proper starting point for any discussion of race; if I did get it, I would feel the other "it," the anger that is like an unscratchable itch, one as difficult to put into words as the effect of a child's death, one that a non-Black person will never understand. Oh, but I get "it." I get the feeling that comes with living in a place where so many in the dominant group, if not purposely or consciously racist, don't seem to have a clue. I get it when a non-Black person asks me what it was like to grow up in an entirely Black neighborhood, the implication being that I was raised by monkeys or wolves; I get it when someone wants to know whether my hair would be straight, i.e., normal, if I combed it out. I get why a lot of Black people feel that life's too short to expose yourself to this crap and that it's easier to simply avoid white people whenever possible.

What I don't get, and never have, is why I'm *supposed* to feel that way. I once read a quote from a Black person about Clarence Thomas, a quote that I don't have in front of me but that was very close to "The fact that he gets in bed with a white woman every night tells me all I need to know about him." I want to make it clear that I am no fan of Clarence Thomas, but his sins, to my mind, do not include getting in bed every night with a white woman—or else, obviously, I am a sinner too. What might this sin of Clarence Thomas and Clifford Thompson be? Thinking so little of ourselves as Black men, and, by extension, thinking so little of other Blacks, that we share a bed with a representative of the oppressor? This logic holds only if you consider one person of a given skin color to be as good as another, i.e., if you consider any white person a stand-in for all racist whites, which is the opposite of the creed I adopted in my youth. And this old creed of mine has taken a beating over the years, but it has never given out or, at least before 2014, even threatened to. For every white person who has asked me an idiotic question like those mentioned above, there has been another who has listened to my problems, who has shared his or her own, who has laughed and joked with me, who has, simply put, loved me. (And Black friends have done the same.) Is part of what they love the idea of having a Black friend? You'd have to ask them, but assume for a moment that the answer is yes, and consider that in some integrated situations, Blacks have approached me in friendship *for the same reason.* There are non-Blacks I can't stand the sight of, and there are Blacks I love, and the reverse is also true. It is that simple.

Well, nearly. There are those depressing moments when it seems there is a Black way of looking at things and a white way of looking at things and never the twain shall meet. One day several years ago I was on a fairly crowded Brooklyn-bound subway train whose passengers included a white mother and her inconsolable toddler. What the little girl needed consoling over was not clear, unless it was that her mother, if their display was at all representative, was incapable of impressing on this child that nothing was actually wrong and that therefore the child should, for others' sake if not her own, relax and stop her damn shrieking. Then a man sitting near the two began playing his acoustic guitar and singing to the child, who, surprised into forgetting she was supposed to be upset, stopped her racket and actually smiled. I watched the other whites on the train smile too, as they gazed at one another in shared appreciation of the moment; and then my eyes met those of a Black woman, and we shook our heads, registering the same thought: *This child is being taught to whine with dissatisfaction until she gets her way or the next shiny thing comes along. She is being taught that she is the center of the universe, and we are watching it happen.* And in our exchange was an unspoken judgment on the ways of white folks.

Whites, of course, have their judgments on the ways of Black folks too. Often these judgments are wrong. Much of what ails Blacks is not our fault. Blacks are at an economic disadvantage in this country for reasons including some I've already mentioned, and this puts us at an educational disadvantage: poor neighborhoods do not have the tax base for well-funded public schools and do not have parents contributing extra educational resources, the way, say, Park Slope does, and this educational disadvantage only reinforces the economic one. And Blacks are, there is no denying it, victims of discrimination—conscious or unconscious—in myriad areas of life, from housing to criminal justice to employment. Also true: we do not always help ourselves. Two-thirds of births among Black women are out of wedlock, compared with one-quarter for white women, and according to the research organization Child Trends, "Among Hispanic and white women, 68 percent of all nonmarital births [occur] within cohabiting unions, compared with only 35 and 45 percent, respectively, among black and Asian women." Blacks kill other Blacks at a much higher rate than whites kill other whites. Of course, there are at least two things to consider here. The first is that statistics, even when they're accurate, never tell the whole story; those out-of-wedlock Black births, for example, include the children of my nephew, a sweet man and a very devoted father. The second thing to consider: those critical of Blacks should try being perfect while also being members of a despised minority. If you run into trouble, give a holler.

Where does all this leave us? I can say only where it leaves me: with a finger to point at everyone, I point it with total conviction at no one; unable to fit the crowns of guilt or innocence securely on the head of any whole so-called race, I am back where I started at the age of nineteen, judging people—I say it once more—as individuals. I was back there, at any rate, until the events of 2014.

Twenty-twelve and 2013 had been horrific enough, with young Trayvon Martin followed because he was Black and wearing a hoodie and then shot to death by a man who then went free. As outrageous as Martin's death was, there was some small uncertainty as to what took place between him and George Zimmerman in that land of Stand Your Ground, and even the event at the center of the 2014 Ferguson episode, for all of the ugliness surrounding it, was not entirely clear. Uncertainty, though, was entirely, and painfully, absent in the video showing Eric Garner's death, for which, once again, no one was punished. It was less that incident than what it demonstrated—the blatant lack of justice for Black Americans in matters involving the police and the courts—that made me question the way I had operated in the world all these years. Was my credo, my overriding concern for treating people as individuals in a society tilted against people who looked like me, the mark of a fool? Was it the equivalent of saying "Come on, guys, play nice" in the middle of a war? Or would the abandonment of my core principles in the face of doubt have meant that I lacked integrity?

"Integrity," of course, and ironically, is the state achieved by the process of integration, or forming an undivided whole, and from that point of view, I was not in danger of losing my integrity, since I'd never had any. Undivided? Me, the man who never encountered an issue of which he could not see at least two sides? Even in the face of the blatant horror that was Eric Garner's killing, I had conflicting thoughts—not about the sheer wrong of the police response to a man helplessly repeating "I can't breathe" while his head is pressed to the pavement, but about my own response. I felt something like horror at myself, living as possibly the least upscale member of an increasingly upscale, increasingly white community, basking in my superiority to those ever-engaged in making their petty racial distinctions—this, while the Eric Garners of our nation were being taken from their families and neighborhoods to prison or the grave, largely if not entirely because they were Black. I am friends on Facebook with a young Black woman I barely know, whose posts suggest that she has spent as large a proportion of her life around whites as I have: in the thick of the events of 2014, one of her posts read simply, "I love you, Black people." I understood, oh, I understood perfectly, the feeling behind that post. I had a similar impulse: to run with my arms outstretched to a Black neighborhood, shouting, "I'm sorry! Take me back!" A number of things prevented my doing that, however, of which a couple are relevant here.

First: sorry for *what*, when we get right down to it? For having deprived the Black community of my (nonexistent) wealth? For having denied my people my gifts? (The one day I spent teaching classes in an inner-city public school convinced me, as if I had needed convincing, that that is not where my talents lie.) For having withheld my preternaturally desirable self and the fruits of my grade-A gene pool from a Black woman? (Which woman? Or is there, somewhere, one who embodies all Black women, a kind of sub-Christ? What's Her email address?) *I love you, Black people.* And, actually, I do, in a sense of loving: I love the way, in the face of everything, understanding what we understand, exchanging a knowing glance here and there, we carry on with our lives; I love that in any field of endeavor you care to name, you can find at least one of us, his or her or their presence representing an improbable journey; I love the selflessness with which so many of us care for each other. But that kind of love is distinct from its in-the-flesh counterpart. I cannot claim to love Black people, for the simple reason that I will never meet the vast majority. I love *some* Black people, just as there are some white people I love. All of which left me, once again, where I started, older but no wiser, if anything more confused than before.

My wife, watching me brood, suggested that I participate in a rally that was about to take place in Manhattan; it would help, she said, to be around like-minded people. I wasn't sure there *was* another mind like mine out there—if so, God help the person it belonged to—but I took her advice anyway. She was not able to go to the first rally I attended, which got under way near city hall as the sun was going down, but there was no shortage of people in the park, Black and white and Asian and Latino, shouting slogans into the chilly air—"Black lives matter," "No justice, no peace, no racist police"—in preparation to marching up the middle of Broadway, making the cars and buses go around us. But at another rally, on a late morning in Union Square, where it was colder but sunnier as we took to the streets, my wife joined me. Our voices were two among thousands, indistinguishable but adding to the roar—fittingly, since, as I finally, finally understood, none of this was about my little life. And yet it confirmed for me the rightness of what I had always believed, as people of every shade came together, their color less important than their desire to see the right thing done.

Seventeen Notes on Singing

ON SOUL MUSIC AND
THE PATH NOT FOLLOWED

1.

I was walking on our small green college campus, singing. Dave, beside me, tall and lanky and not known for flattery, said, "You should sing, Cliff." He thought a moment. "You *do* sing, Cliff."

I shrugged and thanked him. "I can sing a little, I guess. I can't *perform.*"

"They could teach you that stuff."

2.

One of my two favorite singers never learned that stuff. A gawky six-foot-one, Otis Redding, who couldn't dance to save his life, would march in place on stage. "If you can't march to it," he once announced with an endearing defensiveness, "it ain't no good!"

3.

The basement of my family's little house held much that my three older siblings once held dear. Along the white stucco walls were stacks of soul LPs and singles. On one red 45 was Otis Redding's "(Sittin' on) the Dock of the Bay"—recorded in 1967, very shortly before his death at twenty-six in a plane crash. I discovered it in the summer of 1975, less than a year after my father died.

4.

For years, "Dock of the Bay" was the only Redding song I knew. I didn't realize it was both the culmination of a career cut short and a departure from the rest of that career. Redding's singing on "Dock" is both soulful and contemplative, conveying the plight of a man who has traveled far in search of something he may well never find. ("Two thousand miles I've roamed / Just to make this dock my home.") His voice is resigned, in contrast, I would discover, to his singing on the records that made his reputation. On his 1966 song "Cigarettes and Coffee," Redding establishes a seemingly calm scene: at "about a quarter till three" in the morning, an hour of quiet dark, a man and woman share cigarettes and coffee while the man talks about their relationship. To this stillness Redding brings urgency, pleading that they go forward together—"If you would take things under consideration and walk down this aisle with me, I would love it, yeah"—the intensity and yearning in his voice rising along with his need to be understood.

5.

And then there is real calm. Also in my family's basement was my big brother's LP *The Best of Sam Cooke*, whose cover featured a black-and-white image of the matinee-handsome, youthful, smiling singer against a yellow background. Yellow is often associated with happiness; on recordings Cooke often seems happy, or at least easy and relaxed. Whether he is reuniting with his love ("Ain't That Good News") or wishing he were back with her ("Bring It On Home"), his voice has an unflappability at its core. The miracle of Sam Cooke is that this quality always fits the mood. When he sings, "If you ever change your mind / About leaving, leaving me behind / Bring it to me—bring your sweet loving / Bring it on home to me," he sounds at once sad about what has happened and satisfied that he has found the voice to say it.

If calm is a constant in Cooke's singing, the texture of his voice ranges from silk to sandpaper, depending on his audience—the mostly white pop fans for whom he crooned or the mostly Black soul fans for whom his delivery took on a rasp. In his more soulful numbers, in that rasp, there is still another quality mixed with joy, one that recognizes joy's darker side.

6.

That side is known to all adults: both the moods that contrast with—and so allow us to recognize—joy, and the amoral nature of joy itself. Sometimes the knowledge is written on faces. I have a photograph of myself sitting next to a male friend; at the time it was taken, we were in our early thirties, and I was the father of a small child. My friend and I, sitting and leaning forward, are both smiling, but I am always struck—what is a personal essayist if not self-obsessed?—by what else is on my face, settling around the eyes: every experience I'd had, everything I brought to bear on raising another, and all that raising another had added to those experiences. I saw the same in the grim smile of another friend as he and I talked in his apartment one evening. I'd known this man since we were young editorial assistants, and I could see, as he sat across his kitchen table, talking about his negotiations with his teen daughter, a knowingness that had not always been there, a quality for an actor to study.

This is the knowingness in Cooke's voice when he sings, "I ain't felt this good since I don't know when / And I might not feel this good again / So come on and let the good times roll . . ."

7.

In my early twenties I shared an apartment with a friend I'll call Lisa. After a few months she moved to a different city, preventing what would possibly, and possibly unwisely, have become a romantic involvement. Lisa, who represented a road not taken, one day rather tactlessly suggested another untaken path: hearing me sing to myself, and having read some of my prose, she asked, "Why writing? Why not singing?"

8.

The answer requires an absurd comparison. Both Cooke and Redding, from young ages, exuded confidence around others, an invaluable asset for performers; I remember a counselor at the summer day camp I attended saying that I was "too quiet." Cooke and Redding grew up in religious households where singing, beginning with gospel music, was simply what their families *did*; Sundays found the members of my household scattered to the winds, and a story famous in our family has it that when I was a baby, my mother came running from our next-door neighbor's house because she thought I was screaming in agony—only to find one of my sisters singing while washing the dishes.

9.

And yet I love to sing. Writing allows one to express what one thinks and feels, but singing, for me, is *all* feeling, guided by instinct to the right notes but otherwise freed from my near-constant companion, rationality. My eyes close; I am lost in sound.

10.

I occasionally fantasize about singing "Ain't That Good News" in a coffeehouse somewhere. But I am happy singing for myself. I don't regret that I never tried to do it professionally. Some ideas may live most happily at the dream stage.

11.

My regret is that I don't seem to do it as well as I once did. As a family man who has not lived alone for over a quarter-century, I do not belt out songs as often or as freely as before, and maybe my singing muscle has atrophied. Maybe after five decades voices just get worse. Whatever the cause, sometimes when I sing now, I hear my voice straying from the right note, like a small child too curious to walk home in straight lines. Has my voice faded? Or is it that my ear has gotten better? None of this would seem to matter, since I only ever sang for myself. But it presents a minor challenge to my sense—which I have carried deep into middle age—of who I am, who I have been, and what I can do going forward. In itself this challenge is not much; yet it seems a harbinger of a great deal.

12.

Why are Cooke and Redding my favorite singers? Why not, say, Aretha Franklin and Whitney Houston, who, objectively speaking, had two of the greatest voices ever to grace the recording industry? Such preferences are mysterious and subjective, but if I had to make a guess, it would involve my father. His death, when I was eleven, was both sudden and not. He had long had cardiovascular problems, which his smoking did not help; on the other hand, his maladies did not fit my limited understanding of illness, and his death, for me, came out of nowhere—one day he was walking and talking like a normal, healthy person, and the next day he was gone. I still had the guidance and heard the voices of the women in my life—my mother, my grandmother, my two sisters—but the chief male voice had been silenced. Is it possible that on some level, missing that authoritative male voice, I craved others, even the disembodied? Especially when those disembodied voices were so beautiful?

13.

One bit of irony is that I soon lived longer than both of my elders Cooke and Redding. Another is that if I really was seeking guidance in the two men's voices, keys to the mystery of how to live, the circumstances of Cooke's death suggest that I was barking up the wrong tree. Cooke's great demon was his libido. Three of his girlfriends were pregnant with his children at the same time. On the last night of his life, in late 1964, he checked into a motel with a woman who turned out to be a sex worker and who ran off with his wallet and pants; enraged, wearing only a jacket and shoes, he went to the motel office demanding to know where the woman had gone, and the manager—who later claimed Cooke had become violent with her—fired a gun at him. The last words of the soul icon were reported to be, "Lady, you shot me!" He was thirty-three years old.

14.

Why do I still listen to these men? Cooke and Redding, who both died young, would not seem able to provide guidance from beyond the grave to a growing boy, let alone an aging man. Yet the work each did in the last year of his life offers a clue for going forward. After years of singing songs whose trademark was their urgency, Redding, in his final recording, offered up a masterpiece of mournful contemplation. Cooke, spurred by a personal encounter with racism to write and record the 1964 song "A Change Is Gonna Come," an anthem of the civil rights movement, traded the calm at the core of his delivery for a tone of restlessness and longing.

15.

When I was a young man and felt I was singing well, my voice followed the style of the singer I'd heard perform the song. On the page, I've never consciously imitated another writer.

16.

Otis Redding admired, and sought for himself, both Sam Cooke's status as a soul singer and his autonomy in the studio. Jonathan Gould, author of *Otis Redding: An Unfinished Life*, observes that fairly far into Redding's career, Cooke's "effortless grace" as a performer "still eluded" Redding; somehow he never learned "that stuff." But we do not turn to Redding for effortless grace—we already have Cooke. Redding's art, at least before "Dock of the Bay," lay in obvious effort, the feeling that he conveyed so strongly through the suggestion that he could not convey it strongly enough.

11.

As people age, their faces become the faces of their families. (In that photo, I begin to resemble my father.) Yet the people become more themselves. They begin to know better what they love. The things I love bring me joy of the kind that shone forth from Sam Cooke; in my desire to embrace those things in the years I have left, I feel the urgency of Otis Redding.

It is the urgency of a young man walking home with his small child. The man is set on his destination; the child wants to stop at every rock, every tree. Leaves have fallen, and the wind carries a chill. Sometimes, nonetheless, the man lets himself stray from the path a little and follow his child, because he never knows what they might find.

Rooms and Clarinets

ON RACE

AND HEALTH

Malcolm X has been on my mind lately. I'll get to that in a moment.

In my early and mid-teens, I played the clarinet, badly. I gave it up after that, and I don't even know where my old clarinet is. But I have another one now, given to me by a friend who found it in her apartment, left behind by a previous tenant; my friend thought of me as she herself was preparing to move out. The clarinet has mostly stayed in my closet, forgotten—until recently. Most evenings at seven, when the clapping and cheers begin for healthcare workers pushing on bravely in the face of COVID-19, I open my window and add to the din, trilling two notes, an open G and F-sharp, until the clapping and shouting and banging wane, or until I get tired. It is in these moments, holding this sleek black instrument, that I think of Malcolm X, who is shown in a famous photograph standing at a window in his home, dressed in a suit and tie and holding a sleek black rifle. Each evening I chuckle at the absurdity of the comparison. Then I stop chuckling, and a sadness overtakes me.

Malcolm was thirty-nine when he was killed in 1965. I am nearly two decades older than that now, but Malcolm will always feel like an elder. On the whole I have always been a bigger follower of Martin Luther King Jr. than of Malcolm X; I am a peaceful person by nature, and my wish, as laughably unfashionable as it is, is for people to get along when possible. But if King were my father, Malcolm would be the uncle whose visits I secretly couldn't wait for, the one who said so many things I absolutely disagreed with and so many others I would dismiss, I know deep down, at my peril. King's message and actions brought out the best in many of us, and it wasn't his fault if they also brought out the worst in many others. But there was something in Malcolm's message—something that kindled an often shaky pride and self-respect, something that spoke to a righteous anger—that touches a chord in most Black people, too, whether they'll say so or not, and many will, quite proudly. (It should be said that King was a more radical figure than many today take him for, and it is not acknowledged often, or often enough, that at the ends of their respective journeys, the two men were not all that far apart ideologically.)

I feel sad because I know Malcolm would feel sad if he could see us now—if he could see this peculiar moment in our journey, if he could see his warnings seemingly borne out. Malcolm dreamed of a separate nation for Black people, scoffing at the idea that we could ever get a fair shake in this one, and the more time that passes, the harder it is to dismiss his view out of hand. COVID-19 is only the latest development that is bad for the country as a whole but worse for African Americans. The number of Blacks who have died from COVID is disproportionate to the percentage of Blacks in the nation. That is partly because many Black people have preexisting health conditions and jobs that expose them to the public; that, in turn, is because people of color are often lower down on the economic totem pole, and the many reasons for *that* share a root cause, which is racism.

For many years now, more than seem possible to me, my wife and I have shared a two-bedroom apartment in Brooklyn. This is where we raised our children, who are now grown and living elsewhere. And this is where, for two and a half months and counting, we have spent nearly all of our waking hours and seen only each other. Until I was eighteen, I lived in the same house, but when I think of that house, what I picture is the view from my bedroom window of the one across the street; similarly, when I think of my current home, it is not my own face I see but my wife's, and she would probably say the same about me. Racially, we are sort of a microcosm of the country, or of what the country would be if its Black-white ratio were slightly different and its different groups cared more about one another.

We go quietly about our days. Much of my work pre-COVID was already done at home, so our current life has not been a huge adjustment for me that way. My wife's work has been more affected by her having to be here. She manages. We manage. I get up early and read and listen to music until she wakes up. We greet each other with tight hugs and then have coffee in bed. Then we mostly go to separate parts of the apartment, seeing each other occasionally, checking in over dinner about our respective days. Sometimes we watch movies together in the evenings. Comedies are great during this time. I can recommend, if you haven't seen it, Frank Oz's *Bowfinger*, with Steve Martin and Eddie Murphy—I hadn't heard my wife laugh like that in weeks. Other nights, she watches documentaries while I paint in the same room, an arrangement we both like. It's not ideal—I miss movies in a theater, bookstores, bars, my local diners, the Y, art museums—but it's comfortable.

One of the strangest things about our routine, in fact, is how comfortable it is, in contrast to what we know has been happening outside, which of course is death on a fairly massive scale. The closest contact I've had with it are the times when I put on mask and gloves and go to the grocery store, which, during the period when New Yorkers were dying of COVID by the hundreds daily, made me feel like a character on a mission in a World War II movie.

And this weird disconnect parallels what I felt a lot of the time pre-COVID. I live in a very nice, very comfortable neighborhood where there are not a lot of people who look like me, while a lot of people who look like me are in prison—largely because of the so-called war on drugs, a manmade virus that targets people of color. It is not quite accurate to say that I haven't done anything about that or about other issues facing Blacks; I've taken part in protests, I've worked phone banks and knocked on doors during election seasons. But I've done it fitfully, while wondering if it does any good, if my puny and inconsistent efforts matter at all in the face of such enormity.

Like many people in this city where space is at such a premium, I sometimes have dreams—not fantasies: literal nighttime dreams—of finding another room in my apartment I didn't know was there. My wife brilliantly came up with something approaching a real-life answer to this. She placed a little table of ours beside a window in our bedroom; it would not have occurred to me that this little table could hold dinner plates for two, but it does (small ones), and sometimes now we dine there, with a view of brownstones and people and leafy trees, now that spring is here.

I like to think I might also find, not in my apartment but in myself, not rooms, but room—room for more contributions, room for thinking about other ways to make my voice heard. I have written about the issues close to my heart, which can feel like blowing notes into the wind. But perhaps that is the wrong way to think of it. Perhaps is it important to understand that the real enemy is despair, that it is better to find what one can do, with the knowledge that it may not make much difference, than to do nothing.

In the meantime, at seven most evenings, I blow my black horn, adding to the noise. I blow it for those brave healthcare workers. I blow for Black and Brown people in prison too. And a few of those trills go out, though no one hearing them knows it, for Malcolm.

The Quiet Dark

ON FIGHTS, HEALTH,

FATHERING, FILM,

TV, AND LOOKING BACK

On an evening near the end of August in 2021, on one of those late-summer impulses to be free and easy while you still can, my wife and I went to Prospect Park, very close to our home in Brooklyn, for an outdoor showing of *The Black Panther*. We had seen it before, at the time of its 2018 release, in a local theater where part of the spectacle took place offscreen: people who showed their enthusiasm for the film (set in a fictional African nation) by wearing colorful, lavish outfits, complete with headdresses. The scene in the park was a little different. As the sun was going down, families, couples, and groups of friends arranged themselves and their blankets, chairs, food, and beer on the Long Meadow, taking in the pleasant air, the faint smell of bug spray, and the comforting sound of the many amiable and simultaneous conversations. When it was dark, a couple of people got up and spoke with self-deprecating humor, thanking the sponsors and introducing the film. Finally, *The Black Panther* started.

Two things stood out for me in that viewing—one that I had remembered from the first time, one that I hadn't. I had remembered an early fight scene: the title character, also known as T'Challa, the young new ruler of Wakanda, accepts a challenge for the throne from an American called Killmonger. Before a gathering of royalty, elders, and others, the two muscular young men battle bare-chested with swords and shields. In a fair fight, T'Challa loses and is hurled over a waterfall to his presumed death. I was, for the second time, impressed by that plot development. Many are the movies in which the hero suffers defeat, and yet in practically every case, the villain has an unfair advantage, or the hero is outnumbered, or has let himself get out of shape. Rarely does the hero, at the top of his game, simply come up short. For that reason, it seemed to me, *The Black Panther* had called into question the very definition of an action hero, had invited us to rethink the concept. If a hero is not, all things being equal, the one who triumphs, if he is not the strongest person in his own story, then who is he? And why do we follow him?

Then there was the part of the film I had not remembered. T'Challa visits a land of spirits and talks with his deceased father, T'Chaka, Wakanda's former ruler. At one point in their conversation, T'Chaka tells his son, "A father who has not prepared his children for his own death has failed."

I was fifty-eight that summer. My children were grown. Fifty-eight had always been presented to me as an age when many people, maybe especially men, are seized by a wonderful energy. Having reached a stage in life when they know what they want and are, if they're lucky, in a position to pursue it, they are on fire with industry and creativity. This was life's sweet spot, a time for bringing one's remaining vitality and half a century's experience to one's work. I remembered an interview with Gene Hackman from the late 1980s or early 1990s—when the actor was in his late fifties or early sixties, arguably at the peak of his popularity—in which he said he was looking forward to great screen roles in the next few years, before he was relegated to playing grandfathers. In August 2021 I was passionately engaged in my work, but the "grandfather" comment was a reminder of what would, sometime, inevitably, follow. Who could say that I would not, sooner than expected or hoped, encounter my own waterfall? I took the line from T'Chaka to heart. It was time to talk to my children.

I had an opportunity a few evenings later. My older child and her boyfriend came over for dinner. While my wife was in the kitchen, and my daughter, her boyfriend, and I were at the dining table having drinks, I told my daughter that I had been thinking about the line from *The Black Panther* and that, in light of it, there was something I wanted to say to her. I will never forget the look of fear on her face as I spoke, one that said, *I will do anything if only you will stop talking*. I told her, "As someone who has lost both parents, I want you to know: I will always be with you." She understood what I meant—that she need not worry that one day I would simply disappear from her life. As I knew from my own experience, thoughts and memories of me would be with her as long as she herself was alive. I think of my own parents every day, and my daughter would always think of me too.

Soon we began eating, and the conversation moved on to other things. I felt a sense of relief at having, I thought, discharged my duty as a father. (I had already talked about all of it over the phone with my younger child.) After my daughter and her boyfriend left, I went to bed feeling content.

I woke up hours later, around 3:00 a.m., with a ferocious pain in my lower abdomen on the right side. I went to the bathroom and chewed antacid tablets. The pain just got worse, coming in waves. I woke my wife up. "Hey, you," I said, "my stomach is killing me." It felt to me—I don't recall if I said this aloud or not—as if my body was concentrating all of its energy on trying to expel something. After a while I said, "This isn't good. I need to go to the emergency room."

What follows is, in my memory, a montage of brief, not-necessarily-in-order film shots: walking with my wife for three blocks in the quiet dark to the local hospital; hearing the intake nurse ask me from behind a desk for my mother's maiden name; telling her my mother's maiden name while screaming in my head,

Lady, my stomach is about to pop open!; feeling certain that I had appendicitis; telling my wife, as we sat in a hallway near a nurse's station, "I think I may throw up"; being handed a clear, tubular plastic bag; being directed to a cot in a room off the hallway, where someone had not gotten around to changing the excrement-stained sheets; going to a different cot in a different room; dry-heaving into the bag as the TV above blared Ultimate Fighting Championship; having a doctor feel my stomach and back and say that a kidney stone could be causing the trouble; taking morphine pills; being wheeled feet-first on a gurney to a room where my abdomen would be scanned; hearing the doctor say that, in fact, I had a kidney stone; walking home in daylight.

Over the next few early September days, I took morphine and waited for the stone to pass (which happened painlessly and without my knowledge). Otherwise, I simply convalesced, propped up in bed and watching a lot of TV. After my painful wakeup call regarding age and mortality, I wanted the visual equivalent of comfort food. For me, that meant old episodes of *Star Trek*. During high school, in the 1970s, I had watched many reruns of the original series from the previous decade, and rewatching them now, I was struck by a couple of things. One was that, whereas I had always considered the acting on that classic science fiction series to be simply and laughably bad, I now realized that it actually harkened back to the traditions of a bygone era. The original *Star Trek* series was unique in that its cutting-edge, multicultural casting and thinly veiled, of-the-moment social commentary coexisted with the dustiest of theatrical tropes. The second thing that struck me, as with rewatching *The Black Panther*, involved the fight scenes. Another source of unintended humor on *Star Trek* was how easily and often Captain Kirk's shirt would rip, exposing his beefcake chest. Those scenes sometimes bordered on the ridiculous. (*Wait a minute. The guy swung at him and missed. How did that tear Kirk's uniform?*) That device was no doubt meant to attract women viewers. But it also got me thinking about living, aging, and the concept of the hero.

Kirk's ripped clothing shows off his flesh, but it also shows what Kirk, the main hero of *Star Trek*, has been through. We all want people to know the sorrows life has placed on us—except when it comes to our defeats. I am no different: I was happy to share with you details of one of the more agonizing nights of my life, but as for the serious defeats—well, I don't even want to remember them, let alone recount them to you. Why, though? Why do we want others to know what we've suffered, except when that suffering owes something to our own shortfalls? Why, if we want to recall our hardships, are we reluctant to discuss those times when life was simply too much for us?

Whatever the reason, perhaps this is why screenwriters so seldom give us an action hero who simply, and with no excuses, fails—the theory, I guess, being that we want to spend two hours escaping our miserable lives and identifying with someone who is superior to ourselves. Let's assume for the moment that this is accurate. What, then, keeps us interested in our own lives—those of us, that is, who cannot claim never to lose except when confronted with disadvantages? What maintains our view of ourselves as (to borrow a phrase from *David Copperfield*) the heroes of our own lives? I have never had what has come to be called suicidal ideation, and so perhaps it is inappropriate for me to speculate, but I wonder whether at the bottom of some suicides is the thought *This character is all wrong for this story.*

For those who might rather be dead but don't want to kill themselves, there is this consolation: one day, something will do the job for you. That thought is hard to avoid when one is coming up on sixty and finds oneself in the emergency room with a kidney stone. I've also noticed an increasing tendency, during my dimmer moments, to consider my life as a whole in terms of victory or defeat. I wonder if some part of the desire to be a father (as opposed to a mother, because this is the kind of stupidity men are capable of) is the wish to leave behind those who can succeed where we have failed—the equivalent of making a pass in basketball when we ourselves are unlikely to score.

I don't know the answer to that. I do know that lately, as often as not, when I wake up in the morning, in the quiet dark, with the trees seen through the window in relief against an unlit colorless sky, I feel a deep sadness over something I can't quite name. My working theory is that I'm feeling an awareness of eventual death, mine and those of the people I love, a feeling that may simply come with aging, helped along, no doubt, by something like a kidney stone. I lie in bed a few minutes, thinking about the things I'm excited to do in the hours ahead, and some of that late-fifties energy takes hold, and before long I'm up. I will meet the day, whatever comes of it. It is all we can ask of ourselves, maybe all we ought to ask of our heroes.

Preparing our children for our deaths means, of course, preparing ourselves. We fear no longer being . . . well, no longer being. We fear that the movie will end before we have finished the story, before we have—whatever this means for us—won. To die is to lose in an unfair fight. One of those ganged up against us is time. I wonder if there is solace there, provided we can bring ourselves to accept it. Look at the odds we face. Look at the wins, the losses, all of it. See the montage of our lives, the collage of gleeful anticipation, boredom, the laughter of *I can't believe this shit* and the laughter of joy, beers with friends, illness, our children's tears and our own, our wife's smile, scattered moments of ecstasy, occasional glimpses through the window of the darkening late-summer sky. Look at how far we've made it, and all we've made it through.

Siân Griffiths, *The Sum of Her Parts: Essays*

Ned Stuckey-French, *One by One, the Stars: Essays*

John Griswold, *The Age of Clear Profit: Collected
    Essays on Home and the Narrow Road*

Joseph Geha, *Kitchen Arabic: How My Family Came to
    America and the Recipes We Brought with Us*

Lawrence Lenhart, *Backvalley Ferrets: A Rewilding of the Colorado
    Plateau*

Sarah Beth Childers, *Prodigals: A Sister's Memoir of Appalachia*

Jodi Varon, *Your Eyes Will Be My Window: Essays*

Sandra Gail Lambert, *My Withered Legs and Other Essays*

Brooke Champagne, *Nola Face*

Diane Mehta, *Happier Far: Essays*

Clifford Thompson, *Jazz June: A Self-Portrait in Essays*